The PENSION STRATEGY

THE ULTIMATE GUIDE TO PERSONAL INVESTING

The PENSION STRATEGY

THE ULTIMATE GUIDE TO PERSONAL INVESTING

ANDREW SPRINGETT, CFP

INSOMNIAC PRESS

Interior design by Marijke Friesen

Library and Archives Canada Cataloguing in Publication

Springett, Andrew, 1973-
The pension strategy : the ultimate guide to personal investing / Andrew Springett.

Previously published under title: The pension strategy for Canadians.
Includes index.
ISBN 1-894663-89-6

1. Retirement income--Canada--Planning. 2. Investments. I. Springett, Andrew, 1973- . Pension strategy for Canadians. II. Title.

HG179.S5325 2005 332.024'014'0971 C2004-906910-1

Printed and bound in Canada

Insomniac Press
192 Spadina Avenue, Suite 403
Toronto, Ontario, Canada, M5T 2C2
www.insomniacpress.com

In memory of Gordon Springett.

TABLE OF CONTENTS

Acknowledgements

Thanks to my wife, Jessica, for her love and support during this project—it wouldn't have happened without you.

A large number of people have contributed to my financial education over the years—thanks for taking the time. I'd like to thank Lorne for taking a chance and giving a young guy his first job on Bay Street. My friends certainly deserve my thanks for all the years they've put up with listening to my ramblings and my parents Gordon and Judith deserve the greatest thanks for doing a great job. Special thanks to Michelle Bullard for sharing her writing expertise, and Mike O'Connor for bringing the project to fruition.

Chapter One

My Quest for a Solution

When you fail to plan you plan to fail.
—Rev. Dr. Robert Schuller

In the spring of 1987, my parents made a decision. Their house was paid for, they had good jobs, but they were missing out on the terrific gains being made in the stock market. Friends and co-workers were telling them how easy it was to make money with mutual funds. They feared they were being left behind.

My parents discussed it very seriously, finally calling my sister and me into the living room to tell us the big news. They sombrely explained to a very young Melissa and Andrew, that they were in their mid-forties, had no pension plan and that if they didn't do something soon, it would be too late.

By the fall of 1987, it was evident to both my sister and me that something was wrong in the Springett household. My parents, nice people who'd never read the business section in their lives, were suddenly poring over stock tables on a daily basis. The atmosphere during these reading sessions became more intense with each passing day. My father started to have trouble sleeping and by early November, we became used to hearing the TV being turned on in the small hours of the night. Soon it was time for another family meeting.

The meeting started and ended quickly. "We can't afford to lose any more money," my father said without preamble. "If we sell the mutual funds now, we can afford to make the mortgage payments. If they go down anymore, we'll have to sell the house."

After that articulate explanation, my father proceeded to pick up the phone and give the instructions required to keep a roof over our heads.

After the family meeting was over, I cornered my mother. She was obviously upset, but like any mother, she had trouble putting off a son asking well-intentioned questions. The details of our situation quickly emerged. The mutual fund salesperson my parents had been referred to thought we had too much equity in the house. He'd explained the considerable tax advantages of borrowing against the house to fund a retirement plan and had put together a strategy for my parents whereby they'd borrow against the full value of the house to buy mutual funds. The payments on our new mortgage would come from the earnings produced by the mutual funds.

The plan was simple and it worked well for a few months. Then the markets dropped and with them, the value of many mutual funds. Within a month of the crash, my parents had to make a choice: sell the mutual funds and begin making payments on a new mortgage at the tender age of forty-two or hold on and risk having to sell the house if the markets declined further. They chose the former.

A one-income family with two teenagers once again had mortgage payments to make. Like millions of others, my parents managed, but sacrifices had to be made. The retirement plan, such a cause of excitement a few short months earlier, was the first casualty of the new mortgage. A second casualty quickly emerged, in the form of college tuition for my sister and me. This experience affected my life and direction in a profound way. My parents are smart people; they look both ways before crossing the street. How could this have happened to them?

I've dedicated the majority of my professional life to understanding what happened to my family and to helping families avoid this and the myriad of other financial pitfalls that exist in America. Now, years later, I understand how these events transpired and how they could've been avoided, as well as how things should have turned out. I'd like to show you the proper way to achieve that which eluded my parents: a secure pension.

Historically, most people fail to meet their investment goals. In fact, only about eleven percent of individuals manage to achieve the objectives of their investment program. On the other hand, large investors, such as pension funds, manage to meet their investment goals about ninety percent of the time. That's a huge difference!

My parents failed to meet their financial goals, in spectacular fashion I might add, but they're not alone. Literally millions of Americans have had or will have the same experience. It's a sorry state of affairs, made even worse because it's entirely preventable. Thus began my quest to understand why pension plans have more than eight times the success rate of individuals.

What I uncovered during the course of my investigation surprised me. Pensions are managed by regular people, not brain surgeons or rocket scientists. Pension managers don't spend all day glued to investment reports or reading research on stocks. What is it that they do then? Pension managers follow a simple, but disciplined, process. That's it. They don't work to reinvent the wheel. The managers of the greatest pension funds simply know what works, and that's what they do.

So why didn't my parents succeed?

When my parents borrowed against their home to buy mutual funds, that's what they got. Not a pension plan, but a portfolio of mutual funds.

Think of the people you know who have a strong, secure pension plan, perhaps a teacher, a friend or relative who's a member of a good union or someone who chose to serve our great country through public service. Do they ever worry about their pension suddenly disappearing? I don't think they do. They may not be wealthy when they retire, but they don't lose too many nights' sleep either. That, in a nutshell, is the great benefit of a sound pension plan: peace of mind. People who have a good pension in place, don't worry about what the stock market is doing, and they don't check their statements every month. In fact, I'd bet that the vast majority don't even know what the liquidation value of their pensions is. They don't care. All they know, and in fact all they need to know, is that as long as their contributions are made every year, they'll be well taken care of when that magical retirement day finally comes. Every plan is different, but for the most part, the beneficiaries of these plans can count on sixty to seventy percent of their income to continue for the rest of their lives. I choose to refer to these fantastic vehicles as "the great pension plans."

Now I'm not suggesting that you should consider a career change. I just want to make a point: for a lot of people, a good pension plan can bring peace of mind. I think we all deserve the simplicity, peace and security that a good pension can supply. In this book, I'm going to show you how to create your own personal pension plan. If you're willing to invest a few hours to read this book and two or three hours per year after that, you can have a pension plan, built just for you, that can deliver peace of mind, security and simplicity. Your own private pension will also offer you unparalleled flexibility.

What do flexibility, peace of mind and security add up to? In a word: freedom. The freedom to do the work that ignites your passions; the freedom to retire a little earlier, or perhaps a lot earlier, then you ever thought possible. Freedom is all about working by choice, not out of necessity.

Summary

• Most Americans desire a secure pension to provide security for their family; they just don't want to know about the details.

• Behaviour is an important component of any investment plan. Bad investor behaviour can be more dangerous than bad investments.

• Financial mistakes can have devastating and unexpected effects on family life.

• Being educated doesn't protect you from costly investment mistakes. Intelligent, well-educated people make potentially devastating investment decisions everyday.

• Historically, most people fail to meet their investment goals. Only eleven percent of individuals manage to achieve their objectives, while large investors, the institutional pension funds, successfully meet their investment goals about ninety percent of the time.

• Pension funds are managed by regular people who follow simple, but disciplined, procedures. They know what works and that's what they do.

• In a nutshell, the great benefit of a sound pension plan is peace of mind.

• The beneficiaries of the best pension plans are typically free from financial worry. They can count on sixty to seventy percent of their employment income to continue for the rest of their lives. I choose to refer to these fantastic vehicles as "the great pension plans."

• In this book, I'm going to show you how, in just two or three hours per year, you can build and manage your own personal pension plan. Your own pension will offer you flexibility, peace of mind and security—or in a word, freedom.

CHAPTER TWO

What Is a Pension Plan?

Waste neither time nor money, but make the best use of both.
—Benjamin Franklin

A pension is a lifetime payment commencing after retirement that lasts until the death of the beneficiary or their spouse. The pension plan itself is nothing more than the mechanism for managing the pool of money required to make good on promised payments.

Public pensions have existed since the eleventh century, originally introduced in China under Emperor Wan An-shih. Life expectancy wasn't very long, so these plans were, and for that matter still are, very simple. Either the company or the worker would contribute a portion of wages to the government every month. In exchange, the government agreed to pay the worker a fixed amount each month once the person was too old to continue working.

The essence of this type of plan is very basic. Money is being loaned to the government; the government has the use of this money for its own purposes. At the time of the pension owner's retirement, the money is repaid in small monthly payments. In this type of pension plan, there's no common pool of money. In fact, there's no separate pension money at all! The government simply adds the contributions to its treasury and uses them as it sees fit. When the time comes to make a pension payment, it simply takes that money out of the current treasury.

Why the history lesson? It's important to differentiate between a government pension and a pension plan. In today's vernacular, there's a tendency for people to view these two distinct entities as the same. In a government pension scheme, there's no planning and no plan. Money contributed today, by a company or person, is used by the government today to meet current government obligations. Future pension payments are treated as current obligations of the government at the time they're paid.

Private pension plans, on the other hand, are relatively new. In 1874, Canadian-based Grand Trunk Railway became the first North American company to offer a private pension plan to its employees. In 1875, the American Express Company followed suit, becoming the first American company with a private pension plan.

Private pension plans differ from public pensions in one very notable way; private plans pool the contributions made by employers and employees. This pool of money is put to work on behalf of its future beneficiaries. Because this pool of money is growing and compounding, the contributions required are significantly less than those required by a public plan.

Earlier, when I used the examples of a teacher and a government employee, I didn't highlight that the teacher belongs to a private pension plan, while the government employee is simply entitled to receive a pension payment from the government's regular budget. There was a reason for this. The main benefits to both types of plans are the same—peace of mind, simplicity and security. Both government pensions and private pension plans deliver the same things to those fortunate enough to own them. How they go about delivering them is the only real difference. The government pension makes its pension payments from the regular budget of that government. The private pension plan, however, makes its pension payments from the earnings it's generating. Because the contributions made to a private pension plan are working for its members, the amount of contributions or savings required is significantly lower.

I'm sure you're familiar with many examples of great private pension plans. Police officers have great plans, as do fire fighters, auto workers and most unionized employees. The point I want to drive home is that these plans all have one thing in common, one underlying reason why they're so effective. I'll give you a hint—it's not that these plans are kept afloat with huge financial contributions; employers simply lack the will and the financial resources for huge contributions. The one thing all private pension plans have in common is that they make the pension money work for them. In fact, they work this money to the bone. Money in and of itself is neither good nor evil; money is not safety nor comfort and it certainly can't buy love. Money is what money does. I can't state it any more simply than that. Money is simply a tool to deliver those things we find important for ourselves and our families, such as security and peace of mind. If you think I just contradicted myself, then I politely suggest you reread this paragraph because you've missed the point. Private pension funds simply use the money contributed as the tool it is. They use this tool to build a bright, secure and comfortable future for their owners, and from the owners' perspectives, they do it in the simplest way possible. The members of the plan make their contribution, and when they're ready to retire they receive a safe and steady income, which increases with inflation for the rest of their lives.

Unfortunately, most private pension plans are designed for people who earn average amounts of money. If you earn an above-average living and want to continue that lifestyle into retirement, or if you're not fortunate enough to belong to one of the "great pension plans," then it's time to put together one of your own.

The purpose of this book is not to concentrate on what these great pension plans do, but rather to concentrate on how they do it. There are over 3,000 private pension plans in North America. Three thousand private pension plans and they're all managed the same way although, the exact technique can vary a little from plan to plan. Laws can differ, some plans are new and don't have any retired members yet and some have an older membership, but the management strategy never wavers. The basic tenets that cover the teachers' plan are the same as those that govern the autoworkers or the cops or the plan to which the nice man who fixed your broken pipe last year belongs. The one thing that all private pension plans have in common is, simply put, a plan. And the name of that plan is the same for all 3,000+ pensions out there. It's called modern portfolio theory.

Summary

- A pension is a lifetime payment, commencing after retirement, that lasts until the death of the beneficiary or their spouse.
- The pension plan itself is nothing more than the mechanism for managing the pool of money required to make good on the promised payments.
- Public pensions have existed since the eleventh century. Either the company or the worker would contribute a portion of wages to the government every month. In exchange, the government agreed to pay a fixed amount each month, once the person was too old to continue working.
- It's important to differentiate between a government pension and a private pension plan. In a government pension scheme, there's no planning and no plan. Private plans pool the contributions made by employers and employees.
- Private pension plans put the pool of contributions to work on behalf of future beneficiaries. Because the pool of money is growing and compounding, the contributions required are significantly less than those required by a public plan.
- All private pension funds have in common the fact that they make the pension money work for them.
- Most private pension plans are designed for people who earn average amounts of money. If you earn more than that, or if you're not fortunate enough to belong to a pension plan, then it's time to put together one of your own.
- All private pensions are based on the tenets of modern portfolio theory.

CHAPTER THREE

Modern Portfolio Theory

No matter how far you have gone on the wrong road, turn back.
—Turkish Proverb

The history of pension plans can effectively be divided into two periods: pre- and post-Harry Markowitz. Prior to 1952, the world of investing was dominated by individual security selection, in other words, stock picking. Investors looked at each investment separately. They considered the potential risk and potential return of an investment and then made a decision. The most important component in a pension or an individual's investment plan, was the skill of the investment manager. The manager could literally make or break the investment plan.

In 1952, Harry Markowitz, then a doctoral candidate at the University of Chicago, published a groundbreaking new theory, aptly titled "Portfolio Selection," in the *Journal of Finance*. Markowitz's work forms the basis for modern portfolio theory, or simply portfolio theory as he prefers to call it, and it eventually led him to a Nobel Prize in Economics.

Portfolio theory forever changed the way large institutions and pension funds managed their money. Markowitz established the concept of the investment portfolio at a time when each investment was considered a separate entity. A portfolio is simply a single pool of investments with a common purpose. For example, you may have several different investment accounts, all of which are earmarked for your retirement. Your investment portfolio would be comprised of all these accounts added together. In

1952, Markowitz proved that an investment portfolio should be considered in its entirety only.

He established that individual investment managers, individual accounts and even individual investments were not important; that it doesn't matter how risky a single stock or a bond is; and it's not even important if a single stock or bond made or lost money. In fact, only two things matter:

1. how much risk the portfolio is taking
2. how much money the portfolio is making

This may not sound revolutionary to you, but it was a quantum leap forward for pension plans.

My goal is to talk to you in plain language and keep things as simple as possible, while teaching you to turn your personal investment portfolio into something as safe, comfortable and consistent as the great pension plans. Given that goal, I don't think the complicated mathematics of Markowitz's Nobel-winning work have any place in this text.

You don't believe me?

Okay. Here's a sample of the type of equation used by modern portfolio theory to calculate the risk of a portfolio:

$$EU = E(R_A) - E(d^* R_L) - V(R_A) / rt + 2^*d^*C_{AL} / rt - d^{2*}V_L / rt$$

If that equation makes sense to you, then maybe you're not reading the appropriate book. If, on the other hand, you got a bit of a sinking feeling when you saw that equation, then relax, because you're in the right place. It's my firm contention that it is utterly and completely unnecessary for you to waste even one moment trying to understand the mathematics behind portfolio theory. It took a Nobel prizewinner to develop it; I think it's safe to say that it would take at least a solid grounding in mathematics and economics to understand it. Fortunately, there are dozens of great software programs that can do this stuff. In fact, one of them was even developed by William Sharpe, co-winner of the Nobel Prize in Economics. If you're starting to get that sinking feeling again, not to worry; you're not going to have to buy any software, and you certainly aren't going to be crunching numbers or performing calculations. That's what a financial advisor is for.

I said before that this concept was a quantum leap forward for pension plans. Why? The entire landscape of the pension world changed after portfolio theory was accepted. Pension plans and the people in charge of them realized for the first time that the risk they were taking was a quantifiable, knowable thing. Of course, they still didn't know the risk for each investment, but once they made the all-important paradigm shift and started considering all the investments together as an investment portfolio, they suddenly knew precisely how much risk they were taking. If all this talk about risk is making you nervous again, take a deep breath and relax. Risk is the key to everything and we'll talk about it in more detail in a future chapter. Why is risk the key to everything? Not for the reasons you may be thinking.

Risk doesn't keep people up at night and risk doesn't lose people money; bad investment plans do those things. All risk does is describe the chance that you won't reach your goal. If your goal is a three percent return, then there's no risk. You can simply buy a government T-bill that you know will pay the desired three percent, while guaranteeing the return of your investment in ninety days. As your investment goals increase, however, risk starts to come into play. I think intuitively we all know that if your goal is a fifteen percent return this year, there's a very real possibility that you won't meet this goal. That chance is your risk.

Markowitz bases modern portfolio theory on the assumption that all investors would like to avoid risk whenever possible. I certainly think that's a fair assumption. In fact, I'd be willing to bet that given the choice between several portfolios all returning ten percent, you'd pick the portfolio with the lowest risk. I know I would. But what about the reverse? If you had your choice between several investment portfolios that were all low risk, which one would you pick? I'd bet that you'd select the portfolio with the highest level of return.

Now I want you to stop and read that last paragraph again.

Harry Markowitz's modern portfolio theory, the theory that he was awarded the Nobel Prize for and that every modern-day pension plan treats as its bible, is really just that simple. Congratulations, you're starting to understand how pension managers think.

Markowitz actually phrased his theorem a little differently than I just did. He said:

1. For any level of risk (volatility), consider all of the portfolios that have that volatility. From among them, select the one that has the highest expected return.
2. For any expected return, consider all the portfolios that have that expected return. From among them, select the one that has the lowest volatility.

Markowitz stated that these two definitions are the same. If you aren't sure, read them again. Markowitz reversed his theory, just as I reversed the question a few paragraphs ago. The meaning is the same both ways and was, and still is for that matter, earth shattering: *risk and return are different sides of the same coin.*

Once we know how to precisely measure the amount of risk in your investment portfolio, that risk tells us what return to expect. This is the pivotal concept in pension planning. It began in 1952 as a theory, but it is now known to be an immutable law, no different than the law of gravity. The law of gravity says that what goes up, must come down. The law of pension management says that at the level of risk you're most comfortable with, there's only one investment portfolio that will give you the highest expected return. Or alternatively, if there's a specific return you need to produce, then there's only one investment portfolio that can produce it with the lowest possible risk.

Later in this book, we'll look at the specific investments that would go into each portfolio and how those investments will be allocated and managed. At this point, we have to be careful not to get ahead of ourselves.

If you want to have a safe, comfortable personal pension plan, then you need to understand the concept behind the law of pension management. Stated simply, *there is an investment portfolio that is optimal for you.*

More than that, there's only one portfolio that's optimal for you. Understand, of course, that your optimal portfolio will be different than mine, your friends' and your neighbors'.

The purpose of this book is to help you to find that optimal portfolio, and I promise that if you invest the time to finish reading this book, you'll find it. Investors who don't base their decision-making on portfolio theory worry about a lot of things. They worry about what stocks are doing; they worry about what interest rates are doing; they worry about commissions, fees and expenses; they wonder if it's time to buy or sell. They're missing the big picture, putting the cart before the horse, so to speak. There's only one best portfolio for them! Unless they're fortunate enough to simply stumble onto that portfolio, they could either increase their expected returns without changing the risks they're taking, or they could dramatically cut their risk without giving up any potential returns. The owners of pension plans, on the other hand, don't worry about any of these things (at least not as much). They're invariably comfortable with their plans because they know that as long as they can properly control their behaviour and stick to the plan, their future is secure. Over the long term, their plan will do exactly what it was designed to do, nothing less and nothing more. On the infrequent occasions when owners are required to tend to their plans, the only action usually required is a gentle nudge to ensure that the portfolio is staying on the prescribed course.

I can almost hear you saying, "Yes, but how do I know what my optimal portfolio looks like?" To find your ideal portfolio, we use another staple of the pension world: the efficient frontier.

The Efficient Frontier

Pension funds commonly use portfolio theory and the efficient frontier to fashion an "optimal portfolio" from a universe of risky investments. It's no secret that pension plans have to make payments to their retired members. The managers of these plans consider these payments as obligations. Pensions have both current obligations (to former employees who are retired) and future obligations (to current employees who will be retiring at some point in the future). Pension managers carefully consider the cost of these obligations and establish a return goal. This is the return necessary to ensure that all members of the plan will receive the monthly pension they were promised. The managers of the plan look through all the possible portfolios that can be expected to produce that return. How do they choose a specific portfolio? If you've been paying attention, then you know this is the easy part. The managers simply select the portfolio with the lowest risk that will provide the required return.

Many people assume that pension plans try to make as much money as possible. This couldn't be farther from the truth. Pension plans have only one simple goal: take as little risk as possible, while achieving the required return. In other words, their goal is to be efficient. If your goal is to make as much money as possible, you don't have a goal. What you have is an accident waiting to happen. I'm sure you know someone who has lost a significant portion of his or her investment portfolio over the past few years. It may even be that you have experienced a significant loss personally. Virtually all of these people have something in common: they didn't know exactly how much risk they were taking. Forget a properly designed portfolio with the lowest possible amount of risk for their return goal; they didn't even know what was at risk! This situation is sad, because it's so easily preventable. You have to know how much risk you're taking, not approximately, but exactly. If you know the risk, you have a very good idea of the return.

The stewards of the great pension funds know this. They realize that if their goal is an eight percent return, there's a portfolio that can be expected to provide this with the lowest possible level of risk. They know the same is true for nine or ten, even twelve or thirteen percent and all points in between.

The efficient frontier is simply the line that represents each one of these points on a graph of risk versus return. Please take a moment to look at Figure 1.

EFFICIENT FRONTIER (FIG. 1)

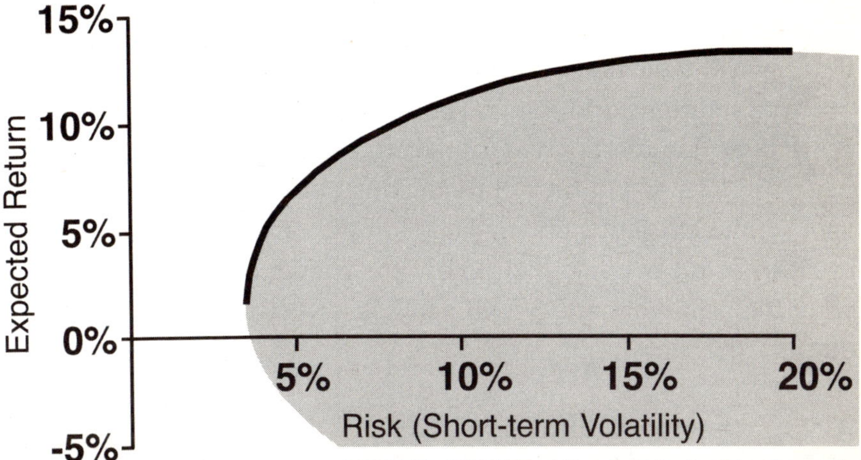

SOURCE: CIBC Wood Gundy Private Client Investing

The dark region is the achievable risk-return space. For every point in that space, there's a portfolio that can be easily constructed from the universe of available investments. Just for fun, pick a point in the dark region of the graph. Put your finger on the point you picked. Now look at the graph. If you look directly above your finger, you should be able to see a better portfolio. There's a point within the achievable risk-return space where you could have a higher return with the exact same amount of risk. If you look to the left of your finger, you should also be able to see a point that could be expected to provide you with the exact same amount of return, but with a dramatically lower amount of risk.

The efficient frontier is the curve that runs along the top of the achievable region. Investment portfolios that lie directly on the efficient frontier are perfect portfolios in the sense that they require the lowest possible amount of risk for a given expected return and they provide the maximum possible return for a given level of risk. Why on earth would anyone knowingly choose to invest anywhere but on the efficient frontier? Every day, literally millions of Americans needlessly throw away money by taking undue risk. They don't understand the efficient frontier and they don't know the law of pension plans!

The managers of the great pension plans understand. They don't waste their time worrying about interest rates or what the markets are doing and they certainly don't waste their time worrying over the latest "crisis." Instead, the managers of the great pension plans spend their time making sure they're on the right spot on the efficient frontier. They know exactly what their level of risk is, and because they know their level of risk they know what their ultimate return will be. Risk and return are ultimately one and the same.

A Note About Possibilities

The models on which Dr. Markowitz's modern portfolio theory is based, are themselves based in part on historical interactions between different asset classes. The past has always been the most reliable indicator of future interactions, however, history does not always repeat itself in exactly the same fashion. Pension managers understand that just because you start with an optimal portfolio, doesn't mean that you'll automatically achieve a perfect result. There are numerous other factors that will affect your return, your behaviour chief among these. In investment planning, it's critical to understand and be comfortable with the real risks you face, as well as the range of possible returns. If you're comfortable, it'll be much easier for you to make wise decisions and exercise control over your behaviour. An understanding of what risk really is and what it really means to you is critical in order for you to achieve investment success. The next chapter is devoted to helping you build that understanding.

Summary

• In 1952, Harry Markowitz published a groundbreaking new theory titled "Portfolio Selection." Markowitz's work forms the basis for modern portfolio theory. This work eventually led him to a Nobel Prize in Economics.

• The history of pension plans can effectively be divided into two periods: pre- and post-Harry Markowitz.

• Markowitz established the concept of the investment portfolio. A portfolio is simply a single pool of investments with a common purpose.

• According to modern portfolio theory, the performance of any single investment is unimportant. What is important is

1. the amount of risk the portfolio is taking
2. how much money the portfolio is making

• Under modern portfolio theory, risk is the key to everything. When all investments are considered together as an investment portfolio, risk becomes a quantifiable, knowable thing.

• Risk is defined as the chance you will fail to achieve your goal.

• Markowitz based modern portfolio theory on the assumption that all investors would like to avoid risk whenever possible. He said:

1. For any level of risk (volatility), consider all of the portfolios that have that volatility. From among them, select the one that has the highest expected return.

2. For any expected return, consider all the portfolios that have that expected return. From among them, select the one that has the lowest volatility.

• Markowitz stated that the two definitions above are the same. Risk and return are different sides of the same coin.

• The law of pension management says that at the level of risk you're most comfortable with, there's only one investment portfolio that will give you the highest expected return.

• There's an investment portfolio that's optimal for you. The purpose of this book is to help you find that optimal portfolio. You'll find your "optimal portfolio" using another staple of the pension world—the efficient frontier.

- Pension plans have only one simple goal: take as little risk as possible, while achieving the required return. In other words, their goal is to be efficient.
- For any given level of risk, there's a single investment portfolio that will offer the maximum possible expected return. The efficient frontier is simply the line that represents each one of these points on a graph of risk versus return.
- When modern portfolio theory and the efficient frontier are applied in tandem, risk and return ultimately become one and the same.

CHAPTER FOUR

Risk

The trouble is, if you don't risk anything, you risk even more.
—Erica Jong

If you're anything like me, then the term "risk" is still making you cringe, at least a little bit. There's an old adage in the investment business regarding client motivations. The adage is that every client's decision is based on either greed or fear. I've been around the investing world long enough to say that there's a good deal of truth contained in that rather cynical expression. Greed and fear are just another way of saying return and risk, and the sad truth today is that most investors simply don't fully understand these concepts. Hopefully, you now know that risk and return are really two ways of expressing the same thing. For any given level of risk, there's a corresponding maximum level of return; for any given level of targeted return, there exists a corresponding minimum level of risk.

Before I even began writing this book, I was aware that the chapter on risk would pose a problem. The simple word "risk" strikes fear into the hearts of many people and worse than that, it also has the potential to be immensely boring. I can't think of any other topic that has the potential to instill crippling fear and crippling boredom at the same time. Crippling being the operative term, because to fail to understand risk is to fail to understand return. I'd be doing you a huge disservice if I didn't take this opportunity to make sure you understand the basics. I won't promise that this will be the most interesting chapter in the book, but I will promise you two things:

1. you simply have to know this
2. I'll keep this chapter as short as I possibly can

I say that you have to know about risk because it's quite simply worth a small fortune to you. I want you to take a moment and think about some of the poor investment decisions you've made in the past. Did you really understand the risk inherent in those investments? I'll admit to asking you a loaded question. The answer can only be no. If you'd properly understood the risk involved, then you would've also understood the potential result. For any given level of targeted return, there exists a corresponding minimum level of risk that will achieve it. Why would you have taken on more than this minimal amount of risk? Investors who understand Markowitz's portfolio theory, never expose themselves to excessive risk. Understanding risk is the tool you need to avoid major investment mistakes! And when you stop making mistakes, you'll no longer need to try to make up for them by hitting home runs.

You simply have to know this stuff.

Risk is one of the basic building blocks of portfolio theory. In fact, as we learned in Chapter 3, portfolio theory starts with the assumption that all investors would like to avoid risk whenever possible. My experience in the investment business leads me to the same conclusion, but with one chilling difference: when investors are unaware of risk, they often assume that there is none. Think about your own personal experience. Have you ever been surprised by how your investment portfolio performed? I don't just mean that you were surprised at how much it dropped. Have you ever been surprised at how much it went up? If you've ever been surprised at all, then there had to be a risk involved that you weren't aware of. Remember the other way of talking about the efficient frontier: for any given level of risk, there's a corresponding maximum level of return.

I don't mean to scare you off, but my goal is to teach you how to build a safe, comfortable, personal pension plan. In order to make your plan safe and comfortable, we need to reduce risk as much as possible and more than that, we need to control it. The good news is that risk can be controlled. It isn't even difficult to do, but to do it, you have to understand the different types of risk.

There are five major types of risk that can affect an investment portfolio. As the US dollar changes value relative to the euro and other world currencies, *currency risk* comes into play. *Interest rate risk* can leave you stuck in low-yielding bonds or CDs at the wrong time and *inflation risk* can erode your purchasing power slowly over time. The fourth type of risk is called *specific risk*. As the name implies, specific risk is associated with the risk of a specific investment or a specific investment manager. Specific risk is one of the most dangerous types of risk, but fortunately it's also one of the easiest to eliminate. *Systematic risk*, also known as market risk, describes the movement of the stock market as a whole. There's no way to know if the next ten percent move in the stock market will be up or down, but the great pension plans aren't concerned, because they have their market risk under tight control.

Let's look at the five types of risk in a little more detail. We'll discuss examples of when you might see these risks in real life and how each type of risk can be greatly reduced or even eliminated.

Currency Risk

This is a very real risk for most Americans, but it's one that receives little attention. If you live in the US, you pay virtually all your bills with US dollars. Many people forget to consider, however, that over half the goods we buy on a daily basis are imported. We import everything from fruit and vegetables to clothing, electronics and automobiles. This means that, while we may pay for them in US dollars, the company that imported them needs to pay in the currency in use where the goods originated. If the dollar drops in value, the cost of many of the goods we purchase every day goes up in lockstep with that drop. If the dollar were to increase relative to other currencies, then we'd find imported goods more affordable, however, we'd also find that any foreign investments we own would suddenly decrease in a similar proportion.

Currency risk is even more prevalent when it comes to investing. Virtually all investments are denominated in the currency of the country that issued them. Thus Japanese stocks must be paid for in yen and European stocks must be paid for in euros. Likewise, when these investments are sold, we're paid in that same foreign currency. Mutual funds can seriously confuse this subject and lead investors to miss out on this crucial element of risk. There are approximately 50,000 mutual funds for sale in America. The vast majority of these are denominated in dollars. When we buy a European or other foreign mutual fund and pay in dollars, it's easy to forget about the currency risk, however, just because we forget, doesn't mean that the risk ceases to exist. When you purchase that fund, the manager must immediately convert your money to euros or yen or drachmas—whatever. He does this so that he can purchase the required investments, because of course he has to pay in the local currency. If you purchase a European mutual fund and the fund does well, will making a profit of fifteen percent make you money? It depends on what the currency does. If the euro drops by twenty percent over that period, then you will have made fifteen percent on the investment, but lost twenty percent on the currency, for a net loss of five percent.

Currency risks are very real, but fortunately they can be effectively managed. The easiest way to manage this risk is to keep the majority of your investments in the currency that you use to make the majority of your purchases. If you live in the US, you'd want to have at least sixty percent of your investment portfolio in dollars. What do you do if you dream of retiring to Italy? Increase the euro component of your portfolio in proportion to the amount of your income that you plan to spend in the Europe each year.

The remaining currency risk can be diversified away. Remember that currencies are a zero-sum game. This means that every currency can't drop in value and every currency can't gain.

If you looked at the exchange rates of all world currencies (a huge job, I assure you), you'd find that the average value is always the same. In other words, for the US dollar to gain one percent in value, there has to be a corresponding drop in value in the currency of some other country or combination of countries. If your investment portfolio contains the right amounts of several different currencies, you'll find that any drop in one, will be compensated for by a rise in another. Thus, currency risk can be reduced or even eliminated.

Interest Rate Risk

I'm sure that everyone reading this book is familiar with interest rate risk in one form or another. For example, when you take out a mortgage to buy a house, you might wonder what term to select. People have two primary concerns: being locked in at a high interest rate after interest rates have dropped, or conversely, if they'll be able to afford the payments if interest rates go up. Bonds and Certificates of Deposit (CDs) pose similar quandaries. If we invest in a bond or CD at five percent and rates subsequently increase to seven percent, we've left some serious money on the table. If you were to ask pension managers what they think of that scenario, most will tell you that it's no different than losing money. If we buy a long-term bond or CD and rates go up, we lose money. If we play it safe and rates stay the same or drop, we lose money as well (because we'll be forced to reinvest at a lower rate later).

I like to refer to this phenomenon as the interest rate game. Most of us have played at one time or another. When you play the interest rate game, you're taking a completely unnecessary risk. Remember, our overall goal is to get the maximum return for the minimum possible risk. Pension fund managers know that if they play unnecessary games, eventually they'll lose. You should know this too.

There's some type of risk involved with all investments; our task here is to neutralize that risk. How do we do it with this risk type? We build a ladder and climb over interest rate risk.

A bond ladder eliminates much of interest rate risk by breaking up your investment portfolio into roughly equal chunks of money, invested for different periods of time. A large investment portfolio might have thirty such chunks, with each piece forming a rung on a one- to thirty-year bond ladder. Laddering is a common strategy among the great pension plan managers, because it completely eliminates interest rate risk.

We'll discuss bond laddering in greater detail in Chapter 6.

Inflation Risk

In my humble opinion, inflation risk represents the single largest threat to your investment portfolio. We're all aware of inflation and we all understand inflation, yet very few people plan properly for the devastating effect inflation can have on the real value of their investment portfolio. In the world of investment and retirement planning, inflation is truly the silent killer. If you doubt what I'm saying, you only have to look as far as the nearest actuarial table. An actuarial table is the set of data that life insurance companies use to predict how long an individual of a certain age can be expected to live. We all know that the average life expectancy for a man in the US is about seventy-five, and for the average American woman it's about six years longer. What a lot of people forget to consider is that by virtue of the fact that you're reading this, you're not average. The average includes all the people who perished from tragic accidents in their youth, all the souls taken from us in car accidents and all those lost before their time to diseases. The unfortunate people who die young have the effect of significantly pulling down the average life expectancy. It is after all, the *average* life expectancy.

If you're fifty years old, it's a fair bet that none of these things happened to you, or if one of them did, you recovered. Because of all of the things that didn't happen to you, the average life expectancy no longer applies. Or rather, it's no longer specific enough. To get an accurate idea of how long you'll be around, and thus how long your personal pension plan needs to support you, we need to consider how long the average person—who is your age—will live. Actuarial tables show us that the average fifty-year-old male can expect to live well into his eighties and the average female can still expect to live about six years longer. If you're married, then the odds are that at least one of you will be spending that pension money at bingo well into your nineties.

By the way, new medical discoveries and improvements in medicine are not even considered in this type of actuarial table. If you're younger than fifty, or if you're hopeful of new breakthroughs in medicine, then it's only prudent to assume that either you or your spouse will still be around to see your one hundredth birthday.

Depending on when you retire, it's likely that your investment portfolio will have to support you for at least thirty years. If you're married, or younger than fifty, then forty years isn't out of the question. Over that length of time, inflation can have a devastating effect. Just a couple of years of high inflation at any point in your retirement could permanently reduce your standard of living by twenty to thirty percent. The long-term inflation rate in North America is a little more than three percent. That's not too bad. But even inflation of three percent will increase your expenses by almost 250 percent over a thirty-year retirement. If you're having trouble with this concept, just take a quick trip down memory lane. What did a stamp cost you thirty years ago? What did a movie cost? If you're too young to remember, make a mental note to ask your parents next time you speak with them. It makes for a fun and enlightening conversation.

Fortunately, inflation risk, like all of the five big risks, can be managed. There are several effective tools used by the great pension plans, but they basically boil down to real estate, equities and real return investments. The term "equities" is just a polite way of saying stocks. It refers to the fact that a share in a company entitles the owner to an equity ownership in the company. The vast majority of companies are effectively immune to inflation. As prices and costs rise, companies simply pass those price increases along to their customers. Inflation actually helps many companies, because price increases often give them an opportunity to build more profit into the final purchase price. There aren't a lot of guarantees when it comes to investing in equities, but the great pension plans know that good companies are inflation-proof. You can take that to the bank.

We'll discuss real estate, equities and real return investing in detail later in the book.

Manager (Specific) Risk

In the world of pension fund investing, specific risk relates to the risk associated with a particular investment manager. If you've ever bought a top performing mutual fund only to see its performance lapse shortly thereafter, then you've experienced specific risk. I like to think of it as the risk of a specific manager and for that reason, I like to refer to it as manager risk. Manager risk is best described as the risk that a particular investment manager will underperform the general markets. Specific or manager risk is one of the greatest threats facing most North American investors. Do-it-yourself investors tend to face an even larger amount of manager risk, because they're relying on themselves to fill the role of investment manager. They're taking on a rather large manager risk based on their own skills. For mutual fund investors, manager risk is literally the risk attached to the fund managers with whom they have chosen to invest.

The great pension plans have always taken manager risk very seriously. In the not-too-distant past, mutual funds, banks and insurance companies were derailed by managers who overstepped their bounds. In the late '90s, a trader named Nick Leeson nearly bankrupted 200-year-old Barings Bank single-handedly, when he suddenly lost hundreds of millions of dollars speculating on currencies.

Fortunately, the great pension plans have found ways to reduce and eliminate this brand of risk. Using a process called due diligence, the great planners make decisions based on the performance history and experience of the individual managers they're considering, so the performance of a fund before the current manager arrived isn't generally considered. Additionally, several different investment managers are usually used for each type of investment. By utilizing the due diligence process, the great pension plans realized that they could diversify away manager risk.

When the investment managers in a portfolio are properly diversified the specific or manager risk disappears. Once the first four types of risk facing a portfolio are under control, the only risk that remains is market risk.

Market (Systematic) Risk

Systematic risk, also known as market risk, is best described as the uncertainty of the future value of the stock market as a whole. I feel that the term market risk captures this uncertainty more accurately than the term systematic risk and for that reason, I'll use the term "market risk" for the remainder of this book. There's simply no way to know if the next ten percent move in the stock markets will be up or down. Statistically, it's twice as likely that the next ten percent move will be up as opposed to down, but twice as likely isn't a safe enough bet for the great pension plans.

When Harry Markowitz developed his groundbreaking modern portfolio theory, he became the first person to recognize that market risk could be reduced. Markowitz studied the correlation between different types of investments. Correlation refers to how two or more different types of investments are likely to change in price together. A correlation of 1.00, would mean that the different investments were perfectly related. If one investment was up five percent, the other could be counted on to be up five percent; if one was down eight percent, then you could be sure they'd both be down eight percent.

The lower the correlation between different types of investments, the less likely they are to change price together. A correlation of 0.00 would mean that there is absolutely no relationship between the two investments. When the correlation between two investments is *below* zero, they're said to be negatively correlated. This means that when one goes down in value, you can expect the other to go up. Gold, as an example, tends to have a negative correlation to the stock markets. When the stock markets start to drop, it's likely that gold will rise in value.

Markowitz's discovery of correlation between investments paved the way for a dramatic reduction of risk within pension funds. Prior to Markowitz, market risk was thought to be a purely random event. The great pensions realized that by understanding how the different investments contained within their plans were correlated, they could measure and control the market risk.

Measuring and Eliminating Risk

Learning how to measure and eliminate the five types of risk was the key step that allowed pensions to implement modern portfolio theory and the efficient frontier into their plans. If all five types of risk can be measured, then the risk level of the entire portfolio can be measured and known as well. Remember that knowing the risk allows you to calculate the expected return.

If the risk of an entire investment portfolio can be calculated from its individual parts, then reversing the calculation allows us to do the opposite. That is, if we know the risk level we're comfortable with, we can use the same calculation to determine the exact asset allocation that will provide it.

Learning how to measure and eliminate the five risks takes the hunches and guesswork out of investing. If you need a return of 9.2 percent to fund your retirement, we can now determine exactly how to allocate your investment portfolio in order to have the best chance of a 9.2 percent return with the lowest possible risk. I hope you also realize that we can do the opposite. If you decide that you're most comfortable with a certain level of risk, we can now tell you what the highest possible return you could expect is and what types of securities should be placed in your investment portfolio in order to maximize the probability that you receive it.

The great pensions embraced this breakthrough with gusto. It allowed them to provide the income promised to their members, with greatly reduced contributions and a degree of safety previously unheard of. In fact, according to data provided by RBC BENCHMARK®, Dalbar, Inc. and Lipper Inc., over the past twenty years, the average pension fund has achieved more than double the return the average investor earned, while taking only a fraction of the risk. The pension strategy can do the same for you and your family. The reward is a lifetime of financial security and peace.

I want to thank you for hanging in there. I admit that the topic of risk is easily the least interesting topic in this book. However, as the central building block of modern portfolio theory, it's also the most important. Stay with me; we're almost through it. The only issue left to address is:

How Do the Great Pension Plans Measure Risk?

There are several different ways to measure risk. If you read popular financial publications, you'll often see them refer to such measures of risk as standard deviation, alpha, beta, R-square, shape ratio and Treynor ratio. Fortunately for you, one of these is far more important than the others. Standard deviation is the real key to understanding the risk of your investment portfolio. If you're lucky, you remember learning about standard deviation in high school. If not, don't panic; I'm going to explain it in detail.

Standard deviation describes the probability of the distribution of a series of data. It's commonly referred to as the "bell curve," because when placed on a graph a normal series of data will tend to look a bit like a bell. You should be able to see this in the graph that follows.

THE BELL CURVE OF INVESTMENT RETURNS (FIG. 2)

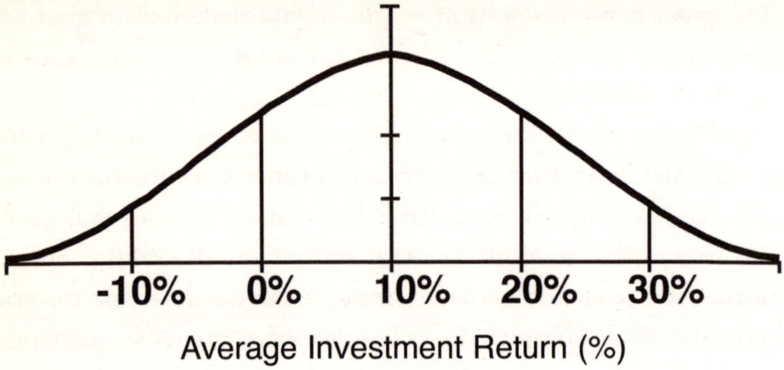

for our purposes. I want you to have financial peace of mind; I don't need you to learn the math. All you need to be able to do is understand what the standard deviation of an investment portfolio means and what can be drawn from it. A fantastic description of how standard deviation is calculated, as prepared by Professor Harley Weston, Chairman of the Department of Mathematics and Statistics at the University of Regina, can be found in Appendix 1 for any of you who're interested or who feel they could use a bit more information to understand this concept fully.

Standard deviation is a unit of measurement expressed as a percentage. For example, a portfolio may have a standard deviation of eight percent. The eight percent represents one "standard" unit of deviation from the average. If the average expected return of a portfolio is ten percent and it has a standard deviation of eight percent, then you could expect that the majority of the time the returns of that portfolio would fall into a range bound by the expected return plus one standard deviation and the expected return minus one standard deviation. Thus, if the expected return is ten percent and the standard deviation is eight percent, then our range of returns would be eighteen percent (ten percent plus eight percent) and two percent (ten percent minus eight percent). In other words, in most years an investment portfolio with an expected return of ten percent and a standard deviation of eight percent would deliver a return of between two percent and eighteen percent. The smaller the standard deviation, the more accurately you can predict what the return of your portfolio will be in any given year.

You may recall that my definition of risk is "the chance that you'll fail to achieve your goal." If your portfolio has a standard deviation of eight percent, then the range of possible returns is fairly high. Your portfolio could make as little as two percent or it could make as much as eighteen percent. What I need you to understand is that as time passes, the standard deviation of your portfolio will drop. The outcome isn't at all random. If you give your portfolio enough time, there'll be exactly as many years when it performs above the expected rate of return as there are when it performs below. As time goes on, the average return of the portfolio will continue to get closer and closer to the expected return.

Most pension plans avoid considering standard deviation for periods of less than three years. The common feeling is that three years is about the shortest period of time over which investment performance can be accurately measured. Given the magnitude of the resources that pensions allocate toward reducing risk, it should come as no surprise that many plans achieve long-term standard deviations below three percent.

For our purposes, you only need to remember two things.

1. There's a sixty-eight percent likelihood that, in any given year, the possible range of returns will be between the expected return minus one unit of standard deviation and the expected return plus one unit of standard deviation. In our example, this means returns will be between two percent and eighteen percent.

2. There's an additional twenty-eight percent chance that, in any given year, the possible range of returns will be wider by another unit of standard deviation. Again using our example, if the range of one standard deviation is between two percent and eighteen percent as above, then there's a much smaller chance that the returns could lie outside that range by as much as eight percent (the value of a unit of deviation for this portfolio). Our lower range is now negative six percent (two percent minus eight

percent) and our upper range is now twenty-four percent (eighteen percent plus six percent).

The two points above may look confusing, but stay with me—they aren't really that bad. Let me summarize what we've learned: In any given year, there's a sixty-eight percent chance that the return of your portfolio will fall within a range bound by one standard deviation. There's an additional twenty-eight percent chance that your return will be within a range bound by two standard deviations.

For our sample portfolio with an expected return of ten percent and a standard deviation of eight percent, in any single year there's a fourteen percent chance that the return would be between negative six percent and two percent and there's a thirty-four percent chance that the return would be between two percent and ten percent. The above-average side is the mirror image of the below-average side, so in any given year, there's also a thirty-four percent likelihood that the return would be between ten percent and eighteen percent and a fourteen percent chance that the return would fall into the highest expected range of eighteen percent to twenty-four percent.

For those of you who prefer a visual of such things, please refer to Figure 3.

USING STANDARD DEVIATION TO MEASURE SHORT-TERM VOLATILITY OF INVESTMENT RETURNS (FIG. 3)

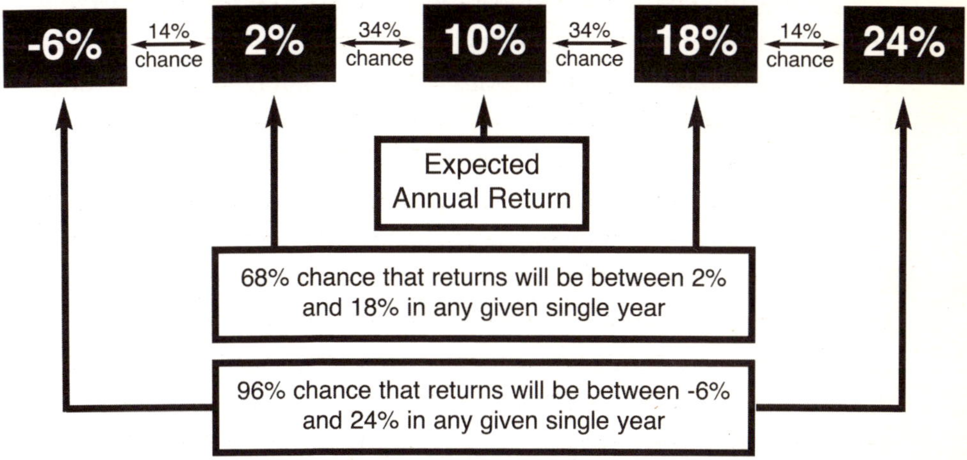

I know there are a lot of numbers here, but please trust that this is important. It's also the only time in this book that I'll ask you to learn anything that looks like math. Please take the time to review the example again. If you have to, read it a third time.

You may be disappointed to see a range of possible returns that's so wide. I know our goal is safe, consistent returns. Don't worry about it yet. For one thing, this was simply an example; your optimal portfolio may require less risk. This would mean a smaller standard deviation and a tighter range of possible returns. The other major reason not to pay much attention to a range of returns this wide, is that we're only talking about a period of one year. With every additional year in which we consider the standard deviation of your returns, your short-term risk, or volatility, diminishes. Most of the great pension funds have long-term standard deviations of less than three percent. Think about that for a moment. Consider what you've learned in this chapter, then imagine what a risk level of three percent would mean to you. It could mean a lot of different things, but foremost it means safety, security and peace of mind. The great pension funds have figured out how to deliver these things, and now that you understand risk you're well on your way to achieving them for yourself. You can start by training yourself to consider risk over progressively longer and longer periods of time.

Taking the chance of being repetitive, I'd like to summarize what you'll be able to do with this knowledge:

• You now understand that risk can be managed. It can be reduced and, in some cases, eliminated.

• You should understand that risk is not a dirty word. Short-term risk is really just volatility; it'll disappear completely over time. Long-term risk is still nothing more than the chance that you'll fail to achieve your goal.

• There's some type of risk attached to *every* type of investment. Just because you didn't know what it was called, doesn't mean it wasn't there. Sometimes there's even risk attached to *not* making a certain type of investment.

• You know that the risk of your individual investments isn't important, because they're not perfectly correlated. What *is* important is the risk level of your entire investment portfolio.

• You now understand that the risk of your entire portfolio is best expressed in percentage terms.

• For you, risk isn't scary any more. It's simply the chance that you'll fail to reach your goal.

By the time you finish reading this book, you'll know how to find out exactly how much risk you're taking. You'll never be surprised by bad returns again, because your investment portfolio will be designed in such a way that you're comfortable with the possible range of returns. You'll understand that with each passing year, the possible range of returns for your investment portfolio will get narrower and narrower. Best of all, your financial future will be safe and secure because you'll know, with a high degree of confidence, what your pension portfolio is going to earn for you and your family.

Summary

• For any given level of risk, there's a corresponding maximum expected level of return; for any given level of return, there exists a corresponding minimum level of risk.

• To fail to understand risk, is to fail to understand return.

• Knowing and understanding risk are the tools you need to avoid making major investment mistakes. When you stop making mistakes, you'll no longer need to try to make up for them by hitting home runs.

• American investors often share a common misapprehension: when unaware of a risk, they often assume that there is none.

• If you've ever been surprised at how much your portfolio gained or lost in value, then there had to be one or more risks involved that you weren't aware of.

• There are five major types of risk at work in an investment portfolio:

1. currency risk
2. interest rate risk
3. inflation risk
4. specific or manager risk
5. systematic risk, more commonly referred to as market risk

• Each type of risk can be greatly reduced or even eliminated.

• The ability to measure the risk of an entire investment portfolio at once was a huge breakthrough for pension investing. If the risk of an entire portfolio can be calculated from its individual parts, then reversing the calculations allows us to do the opposite. That is, if we know the risk or return level we want, we can use the same calculation to determine the asset allocation with the best chance of providing it.

• The great pension plans primarily measure risk using a mathematical tool called standard deviation. Standard deviation is a unit of measurement expressed as a percentage.

• For our purposes, you only need to remember two things about standard deviation:

1. There's a sixty-eight percent likelihood that, in any given

year, the possible range of returns of a portfolio will be between the expected return minus one unit of standard deviation and the expected return plus one unit of standard deviation.

2. There's an additional twenty-eight percent chance that, in any given year, the possible range of returns will be wider by another unit of standard deviation.

- Most pension plans avoid considering standard deviation for periods of less than three years. The common feeling is that three years is about the shortest period of time over which investment performance can be accurately measured. Many of the great pension plans achieve long-term standard deviations below three percent.
- The low long-term risk levels pensions achieve allow them to deliver safety, security and peace of mind to their members. Now that you have a working knowledge of risk, you're well on your way to achieving them for yourself, but you must give your plan enough time.

Chapter Five

Diversification

In the business world, the rearview mirror is always clearer than the windshield.

—Warren Buffett

By now you have a firm understanding of risk. You know that up-and-down movement in your investment portfolio isn't a risk—it's volatility. Risk is simply the chance that you will fail to achieve your goals. You may have noticed that the term diversification came up several times when we were discussing techniques for reducing and eliminating risk. Most of you reading this book probably think you understand what diversification means. I'm here to tell you that, more than likely, you don't. My experience leaves me no other choice. Most Americans think they understand the concept and virtually all of them think they're the owners of diversified portfolios. They don't and they aren't. This misconception has become so prevalent that the term "diversification" has almost become a dirty word. I'm constantly hearing from people that diversification doesn't work. They tell me that they had a diversified portfolio, but they still lost thirty percent of their assets in a downturn. What do these people have in common? They weren't actually diversified.

If you own six different blue chip mutual funds, are you diversified? Of course not. What if you own six different European funds or international funds? Same story. Think back to our discussion of manager risk in the last chapter. Manager risk can be completely eliminated. How do we eliminate it? We diversify it away by using several different managers. So what are these people doing when they split their money up between several different mutual funds? They're diversifying, but only enough to eliminate one of the five risks; manager risk. For the most part, these investors are completely ignoring the other four risks. Being one-fifth diversified is better than nothing, but not by much.

Most investors, and even some investment advisors, pay little more than lip service to the topic of diversification. Yet, if you buttonhole ten pension managers and ask them what the most important techniques behind managing a pension fund are, most likely, all ten will say asset allocation and diversification. The word "diversification" gets tossed around a lot. It appears in almost every TV show, interview or article about investing, but that's not enough to convince today's investors. If you want to reduce risk while improving returns, real diversification is a must. The only way to accomplish real diversification is to utilize all available asset classes in your portfolio.

Typically, the portfolios that make up the efficient frontier are the most highly diversified. Less diversified portfolios tend to be closer to the middle of the achievable region. This can be seen below.

EFFICIENT FRONTIER (FIG. 4)

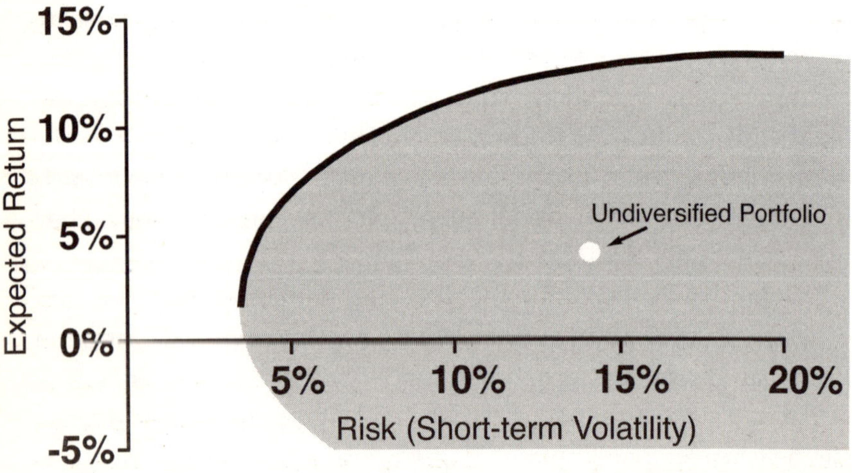

SOURCE: CIBC Wood Gundy Private Client Investing

In order to discuss diversification properly, I need to briefly touch on the different asset classes included in the investment portfolios of the great pension plans. These asset classes will be discussed in greater detail in the following chapter. For now, it's sufficient to discuss them in general terms. The five asset classes are:

1. cash
2. fixed-income (bonds, CDs, preferred shares)
3. equity (stocks)
4. real estate
5. absolute return investments

Most investors grab a basketful of mutual funds or stocks and think they're diversified. The reason their portfolios aren't diversified is that they've only eliminated one of the five types of risk. If we want to reduce and eliminate all five types of risk, we need to use all five asset classes. Why do we need to use all five asset classes? Correlation. The five asset classes each have unique features. They each have their own advantages and disadvantages. Although they can all suffer from price volatility, they don't necessarily do it at the same time. In fact, the very conditions that may lead to a drop in the price of one asset class will generally lead to another asset class enjoying a gain in price. The relationship between the prices of the five asset classes can best be described using correlation.

Think back to the last chapter. Correlation, as it relates to investing, is a statistical technique, which shows how closely two assets are related. Perhaps the best example of correlation is height and weight. Taller people tend to be heavier than shorter people. The relationship between height and weight isn't perfect. I'm sure you can think of a shorter person who's heavier than a taller person you know. However, the more people you take into account, the more precise the relationship becomes. If you considered all the people who live in your city or town, you'd find that as the average height increased, so would the average weight. As you'll recall, this type of correlation is called a positive correlation. You know that on average, as height increases, weight increases as well. Not all events are correlated. The number of people in your city or town who'll buy new cars this summer is completely unrelated to the number of days it'll snow this winter. It's also possible for two different things to have an opposite relationship; you'll recall that this is referred to as a negative correlation. In the case of negatively correlated assets, you could expect that one would go up in price, when the other went down in price, or vice versa.

The correlation between two assets is described by a scale that ranges from -1 to +1. Two assets with a correlation of 1.0 would be perfectly related; as one goes, so would go the other. Two assets with a correlation of 0.0 would be completely unrelated; the movement in price of one tells you nothing about what to expect from the other. Two assets with a correlation of -1.0 are negatively correlated; they'll always move exactly opposite to each other. The effect of any asset class on your portfolio can be quickly and accurately measured with the -1 to +1 correlation scale.

Having assets in your investment portfolio, with a strong positive correlation to each other, doesn't help to diversify it. This is the reason why an investor who owns a large number of equity mutual funds experiences high volatility in his or her portfolio. If some of that same investor's portfolio was in bonds, the volatility would be slightly lower, but because only two asset classes are being utilized, it would still be quite high overall. The same principle applies to a basket of stocks. If an investor has twenty or thirty individual stocks in her portfolio, she may think she's diversified, but since she's only using one asset class, she'll discover that the stocks she owns tends to move up and down with the market. The systematic risk has been diversified somewhat, but the effect of the other four risks will still tend to cause the portfolio to be very volatile.

In order to be properly diversified, a portion of the portfolio needs to be invested in each of the five asset classes. The managers of the great pension plans know and understand this principle.

What would happen to a properly diversified portfolio if the economy suddenly entered a sharp recession? As a general rule, the stock markets as a whole drop significantly during the early stages of a recession. Obviously, the equity portion of a diversified portfolio will drop. The correlation between equities and the stock market as a whole is very high. The cash portion, on the other hand, will be completely unaffected. There's virtually no correlation between cash and the broader stock markets. During a recession, the Federal Reserve will generally lower interest rates in order to help stimulate the economy. Lower interest rates are good for the bonds that a diversified portfolio holds. If the interest rate offered by new bonds is lower, then the value of the bonds already owned in the portfolio will go up proportionately. (We'll talk about bonds in detail later.) The correlation between the declining equity markets and bond prices is generally negative. When stocks go down, bonds tend to go up. Real estate as an asset class also has a negative correlation to declining stock markets. Investment real estate provides a steady income stream; as interest rates drop, the value of this income stream increases.

But how would the fifth asset class, absolute return, react to a sharp recession? I realize there's a good chance that you don't know specifically what type of securities would qualify as part of the absolute return asset class, but for now, let's not worry about it. We'll discuss the absolute return asset class in detail in subsequent chapters. The only thing I'll say about this asset class now is that there's virtually no correlation between the behaviour of the absolute return class and any other class. In other words, none of the many factors that affect the prices of the other four asset classes have any tangible effect on the absolute return class.

Think back to the last recession. The stock markets dropped quite a bit, didn't they? On average, the stock markets drop over thirty percent in a recession. What happened to your investment portfolio? I'd be willing to bet that it dropped as well. Now let's consider what would've happened to a properly diversified portfolio. As the recession started, the equities in the portfolio would've dropped, the cash and absolute return asset classes would've been unaffected by the market drop and you'd expect to see the fixed-income and real estate asset classes rise in value. In total, you have one asset class down in value, two unaffected and two rising in value. The properly diversified portfolio is going to ride out the stock market decline in relative comfort, and if you're the proud owner of a diversified portfolio, you're going to be riding in comfort and safety as well.

Let's try another example. What would happen to a diversified portfolio if we were to enter a period of high inflation? Well, for starters, fixed-income as an asset class is going to get hit hard. High inflation means high interest rates. The same bonds that made us a profit as interest rates dropped are now going to lose money as rates rise. The interest rate we're receiving on our cash will increase, so as an asset class, cash will do well. Equities will not do very well in a high interest rate environment. When investors can get high rates on bonds, they tend to sell their stocks and this pushes the prices down. The real estate asset class will be strong on the other hand; both the value of the properties owned and the income stream from them will tend to rise with inflation. The absolute return asset class will be completely unaffected.

How did our properly diversified portfolio make out in a high inflation environment? The final score was two asset classes down, one unaffected and two up. Note that I didn't say the absolute return asset class finishes even in this example, rather I said it's unaffected. It would still produce something like its expected return. Overall, the diversified portfolio should provide above-average returns in a high inflation environment. The undiversified investor, on the other hand, would be in for a very rough ride. What do most people you know have in their investment accounts? Equities and fixed income—the two very asset classes that were hurt the most. This is a very trying time for average investors. Remember the early '70s?

What about a period of dropping interest rates when the economy is running smoothly? What would happen to the diversified portfolio then? As you might expect, it would do very well. The equities, bonds and real estate would all perform strongly. The absolute return asset class would, of course, be unaffected, as would cash. These periods don't come around very often, but when they do, it's nice. Think about the second half of the '90s. In this type of perfect market undiversified portfolios would also do very well. If they're particularly heavy on stocks, they could even be expected to do better than a diversified portfolio. But you need to remember this: the properly diversified portfolio would be invested throughout this whole period, earning its consistent return. The undiversified investor, on the other hand, may very well still be sitting on the sidelines smarting from the truck that hit his portfolio during the last market drop.

I could go though dozens of examples here, but I think I'm making my point. War, recession, inflation, currency crisis, you name it, whatever the crisis of the day happens to be—parts of the properly diversified portfolio will shine and the ride will be smooth and comfortable. From the peak of the '90s bull market to the bottom of the subsequent bear, the broader stock markets dropped almost fifty percent in what amounts to the second-largest market decline of all time. It was devastating to many investors. How do you think the great pension plans did? I'm sure by now you know the answer. They did just fine. Millions of investors lost literally trillions of dollars in wealth, but the properly diversified portfolios were all right. Why do you suppose that is? I'm not going to tell you just yet; I want you to think about it.

* * *

The answer is, of course, that out of the five asset classes, only one actually went down! Fixed-income and real estate posted great returns and, as you'd expect, the cash and absolute return asset classes were unaffected. One asset class down, two unaffected, two up—just a regular day at the office for a properly diversified portfolio.

Diversifying through the five asset classes lowers the risk and improves the consistency of an investment portfolio. When a portfolio posts consistent returns, there's no need or temptation to take undue risk. A less diversified portfolio will suffer from increased short-term volatility and can easily fluctuate to extremes. The problem with this is that what might seem to be a moderate and acceptable loss at the time will often require a huge gain to offset it. A vicious spiral can ensue, with investors feeling that they have no choice but to take even greater chances in order to make up for lost time.

Please allow me to provide an example. Say you have a less-than-diversified investment portfolio that's expected to return a reasonable ten percent per year. An underdiversified portfolio such as this is exposed to undue and often unwise risk. It would not be uncommon to occasionally see a year posting a loss of fifteen percent. What may surprise you is that in order to make up for the fifteen percent loss, your portfolio would require an astounding forty-two percent gain the following year.

A loss of only fifteen percent requires a gain of forty-two percent in order to get back on track! That's asking a lot. It's not hard to see how some investors are tempted to take unwise chances in their haste to recover losses. On average, the stock market suffers a decline of greater than thirty percent about every five years. The larger the loss, the more difficult it is to recover from. A twenty-five percent decline would require an astronomical sixty-one percent return the following year in order to get back on track. There's simply no way to even attempt to receive a sixty-one percent return that doesn't involve a ton of risk. Taking undue risk inevitably leads to significant losses. Following these inevitable losses, the investor is faced with a choice: they can either accept the permanent setback or attempt to recoup these losses by undertaking more, even higher risks. Ultimately the choice doesn't matter, because this is a train to nowhere—you lose either way. It's time to get off and diversification town is the only winning stop.

The great pension plans understand that diversification is the key to Markowitz's modern portfolio theory. The portfolios that make up the efficient frontier include all five major asset classes, and thus are the most highly diversified. These portfolios can be expected to provide the maximum possible return with the minimum possible risk. Alternatively, underdiversified portfolios tend to deliver lower long-term returns with much more risk than is necessary.

Summary

- Up-and-down movement in your investment portfolio isn't risk, it's short-term volatility.
- Most Americans think their investments are diversified, when in reality they aren't.
- Typically, the portfolios that make up the efficient frontier are the ones that are the most highly diversified.
- A diversified portfolio includes investments from each of the five major asset classes:
    1. cash
    2. fixed-income (bonds, CDs, preferred shares)
    3. equity (stocks)
    4. real estate
    5. absolute return investments
- Because they're not highly correlated to each other, the five asset classes can be used to reduce and eliminate the five big risks.
- Assets with a strong, positive correlation to each other, don't add diversification. This is the reason why an investor who owns a large number of equity mutual funds still experiences high volatility in his or her portfolio.
- During virtually any economic scenario, one or more of the five asset classes will do well. This is one of the reasons properly diversified portfolios tend to experience lower short-term volatility.
- Diversification is one of the keys to Markowitz's modern portfolio theory. The portfolios that make up the efficient frontier are the most highly diversified. Underdiversified portfolios tend to deliver lower returns with much more risk than is necessary.

CHAPTER SIX

Asset Allocation

Risk comes from not knowing what you're doing.
—Warren Buffett

The key pillars of modern portfolio theory are proper diversification and understanding risk. We've worked together to build a sound foundation of understanding for you in these two key concepts. We're now going to put that foundation to work by learning how the great pension plans actually construct their investment portfolios. The great plans design and build their portfolios using the principle of asset allocation.

It's possible that you have some of the same preconceptions about asset allocation that you had about diversification. If that's the case, it's best to try to let go of them right now. The argument in favor of asset allocation is, to put it mildly, overwhelming. In the previous chapter, we learned that there are five asset classes. Hopefully you remember that those five classes are:

1. cash
2. fixed-income (bonds, CDs, preferred shares)
3. equity (stocks)
4. real estate
5. absolute return investments

The great pension plans have been using the work of Markowitz for decades. They've utilized his modern portfolio theory to build safe and consistent plans for millions of people, but perhaps most importantly, they've used his principles of risk management and diversification to provide peace of mind to those same millions. During the course of building and diversifying these minimum-risk portfolios, pension managers started to notice a surprising trend. They noticed that the huge amount of time, energy and money they were devoting to picking the best individual investments just didn't seem to make much difference in the final tally. A professor of finance at Stanford University, decided this unexpected trend was worthy of further investigation. His work uncovered shocking results, and in 1990 he was rewarded as a co-winner of the Nobel Prize in Economics.

What did William Sharpe discover that was worthy of the Nobel Prize? His research proved that in a properly diversified investment portfolio, individual investment selection, market timing and luck were virtually irrelevant factors in the final return. Sharpe found that the single, most important contributor to an investor's lifetime return was asset allocation. Over ninety percent of an investor's total lifetime return can be attributed to this one decision.

CONTRIBUTIONS TO LIFE-TIME INVESTMENT PERFORMANCE (FIG. 5)

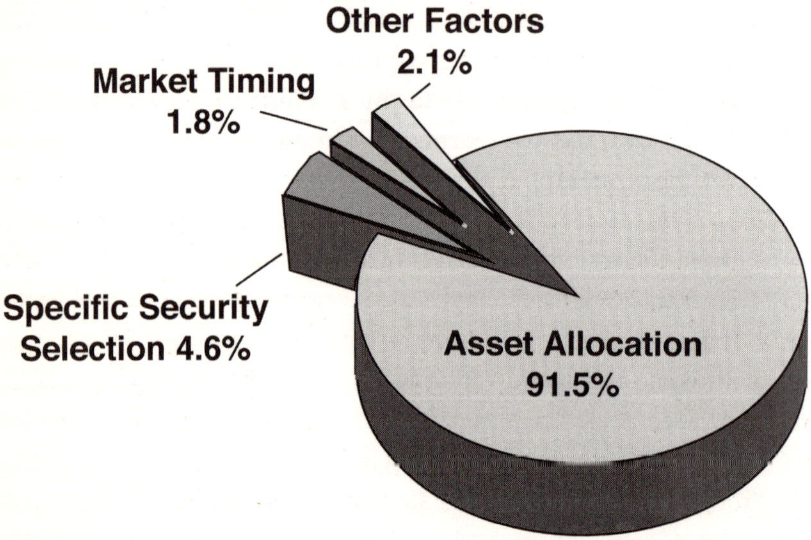

Source: Financial Analysts Journal, May/June 1991, "Determinants of Portfolio Performance II: An update" by Brinson, Singer and Beebower.

Think about your own investment experience. How much time have you spent agonizing over an investment decision? How much energy have you spent deciding if today is the right day to buy? Sharpe proved that these factors are almost irrelevant. The data in Figure 5 shows that the overall asset allocation of your portfolio has almost twenty times more effect on your total performance than your investment selections do. Trying to time the market? Your asset allocation has over fifty times as much affect on your total lifetime performance. Where were you investing your time before? Where are you going to invest your time now? At the beginning of this book, I promised I'd show you how to have safety and comfort, and I told you it would only require a few hours of your time per year. Do I have a magic bullet? No. But I do have modern portfolio theory and I'll assure you it's the next best thing. Together we're going to learn where educated investors concentrate their efforts.

If 91.5 percent of your total lifetime investment return comes from your asset allocation decisions, how much of the roughly four hours per year that most of us devote to our investment plans should be spent on asset allocation? I'm willing to bet you said something like ninety percent. Why? Do you think that, if you spent the other ten percent of your time picking stocks and trying to time the market, it would help? Forget about that stuff. It's a chump's game, not that much different than trying to win the giant bear at the carnival. You may win eventually, but inevitably you realize that you could've bought the bear for less than you spent trying to win it. Why would you want to play a game like that? For fun? Maybe at the carnival, but not with your family's financial security. If you want to risk your money: go to a casino. If you want to provide your family with financial peace of mind: reduce and eliminate risks, diversify and concentrate on proper asset allocation.

I'm going to spend another minute hammering this point home, because it's that important. If the individual investments we pick perform somewhere near average, if we don't try to time the market, if we simply have average luck and we add to that a competent job of asset allocation, then your investment portfolio is going to reward you by earning something like ninety-seven percent of the maximum it could possibly be expected to earn. Now I don't know how you did in school, but where I come from, ninety-seven percent is a very good grade.

Warren Buffett, Peter Lynch and Sir John Templeton are arguably the three most successful investors the world has ever seen. Ask them what they've learned in their long and distinguished careers and you'll find one common theme: you can't time the markets. If you still need more convincing, go out and try to find a professional money manager who thinks the markets can be timed. Do they have more than ten years' experience? No. You can look as long or as hard as you want, but you won't find one, because they simply don't exist. If the three greatest investors in history can't do it, please don't even try. This isn't a carnival game; it's the financial security and comfort of your family you're playing with.

But what about individual investment selection? You may be quite good at it. You may think that, if you put in few extra hours reading research reports and financial magazines, you could pick above-average investments. That would be worthwhile wouldn't it? The answer is that it might be. It might also hurt you. If you want to do it, I can't stop you. I'm of the strong opinion, however, that for most of us, picking winning investments is a losing battle. The chart that follows compares the returns of the average equity mutual fund investor to the returns of the average equity mutual fund. During the greatest bull market in history, the average individual investor cost himself a fortune. He could've thrown darts at the newspaper and made money. Instead, he bought the wrong mutual funds at the wrong times and compounded the problem by selling these at the wrong times to buy more of the wrong funds. It's a completely unnecessary game to play and I reiterate that the people who play this game are playing with the safety and comfort of their families.

AVERAGE STOCK FUND INVESTOR RETURN VS. AVERAGE STOCK FUND RETURN (1984-2000) (FIG. 6)

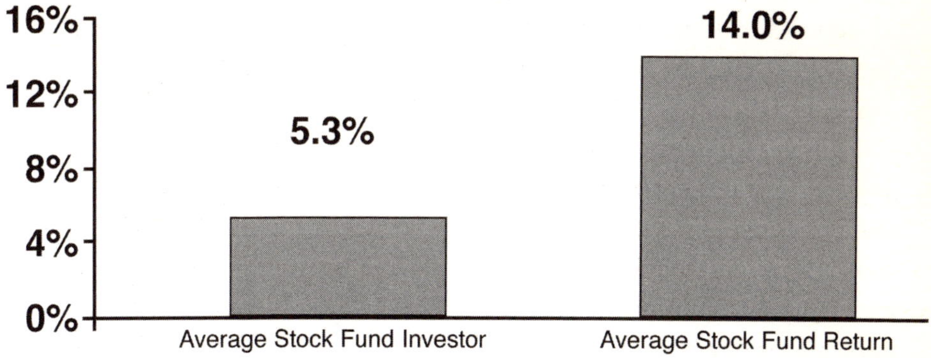

SOURCE: Dalbar Inc. and Lipper Inc.

Hopefully, you've accepted the importance of asset allocation. I realize I'm asking a lot of you. I've asked you to forget everything you thought you knew about diversification and I've asked you to treat asset allocation with more importance than the individual investments you own. What we're doing is making a complete shift in our thinking. The great pension plans made this paradigm shift long ago. The owners of these plans are still being rewarded for that shift in thinking and they'll continue to be rewarded for as long as they live. Their pension plans continue to deliver safety and comfort, but above all, peace of mind. This is what I want for you. If you can let go of what you thought you knew and shift your thinking as the great pension plans did, then you too can achieve the safety, comfort and peace of mind that results.

The next step in understanding the principle of asset allocation is to look at each of the five asset classes in detail. We'll examine the benefits that each asset class brings to your investment portfolio and learn how proper diversification is implemented within each of the five classes. I'll also explain why each class is necessary for the construction of a true minimum-risk portfolio.

Cash and Asset Allocation

I should clarify that for the purposes of asset allocation, cash doesn't refer to the money in your wallet or purse and it doesn't mean shoeboxes full of currency stuffed under your bed. "Cashable" would actually be a better descriptor than "cash." When considering the topic of asset allocation, cash refers to short-term interest-paying investments that are readily accessible. Government T-bills are the classic example. A money market mutual fund would also be considered cash for our purposes. I should also note at this point that, as a general rule, cash is held in the investor's home currency. Most Americans should keep their cash position in dollars. Currency risk is usually best dealt with in the equity and fixed-income asset classes.

The first pillar of asset allocation is always cash—unfortunately the long-term returns on cash aren't attractive. In fact, it's almost a certainty that over your lifetime, cash will be the worst performing asset class you own. One dollar invested in cash in 1926 would be worth about $18 today. Not a great return. If you consider that inflation caused prices to increase by about ten times during that period, it looks even worse. If the effect of taxes were factored in...well, you don't even want to hear about that.

CASH AND INFLATION (FIG. 7)

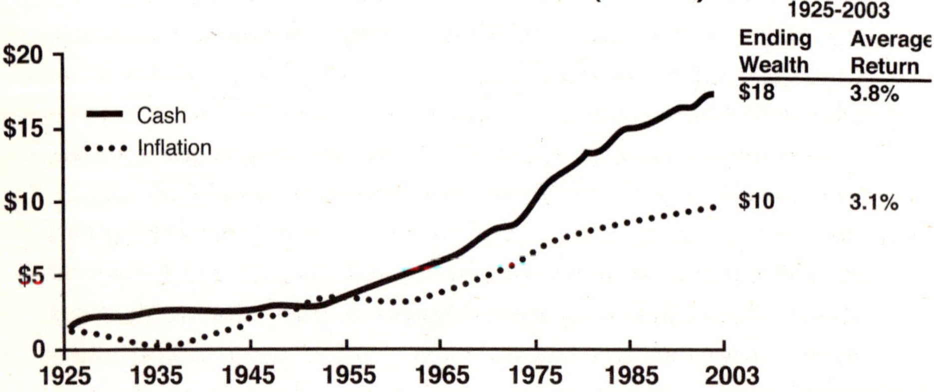

If cash is generally the worst-performing asset class, why on earth would anyone want to own it? The short answer is diversification. During those rare periods when stocks and bonds are dropping in tandem, cash is invariably the best performing asset class. Cash may not have the best long-term track record, but it has been the top performing asset class at times and it will be again. I said that the short answer is diversification. What's the long answer? Peace of mind. In a perfect world, cash as an asset class isn't going to greatly increase your returns. This, however, isn't a perfect world. As an asset class, cash fills two roles: it satisfies your family's need for an emergency fund and it plays a very significant role in reducing the volatility of your investment portfolio. Reduced volatility and likewise reduced short-term risk are crucial to the safety and comfort of your plan. People who feel safe and comfortable don't have any problem sticking to a plan. On the other hand, people who feel panicked are prone to making all sorts of hasty, poor decisions, many of which they'll never recover from.

The great pension managers understand that cash is an important asset class. They realize and accept that it likely won't be the best performer, but they also know that because it's uncorrelated to the other asset classes, it'll significantly reduce volatility and help to keep the plan on a safe and steady course.

Asset Allocation and Fixed-Income

The fixed-income asset class is made up of Certificates of Deposit (CDs), bonds and preferred shares. In this book, I often use the phrases fixed-income and bonds interchangeably. The main concept is that, with all investments in this class, the return is fixed. That is to say, that over the life of the investment, your return is a known, fixed quantity. If you purchase a US Government five-year note yielding 5.25 percent and hold it until maturity, there's no chance that your return will be 6.0 percent and there's no chance that your return will be 4.5 percent. If you hold the bond to maturity, your return will be exactly 5.25 percent. The rate of return is fixed, hence the title fixed-income for the asset class.

Simple enough, right? So why wouldn't someone want to invest their entire portfolio in fixed-income? The rate of return would be known in advance and there'd be no risk, right? Wrong. Think back to the five risks. What risks would apply to fixed income? If you're having trouble remembering, flip back to Chapter 4 where we discussed the five types of risk. It'll be worth your while to reread that section. Believe it or not, all five of the risks apply to the fixed-income asset class to some extent. I'm not as concerned about this as you might think, however. As we learned in Chapter 3, all five risks can be reduced or eliminated. What I am concerned with—no, petrified by—is our overall definition of risk. Remember? Simply put, we defined risk as the chance that you'll fail to achieve your goals. If your portfolio consists of 100 percent fixed-income, what are the chances you'll achieve your goals? Slim to none and slim just left town. The long-term rate of return of fixed-income is better than cash, but it's still terrible.

BONDS, CASH AND INFLATION (FIG. 8)

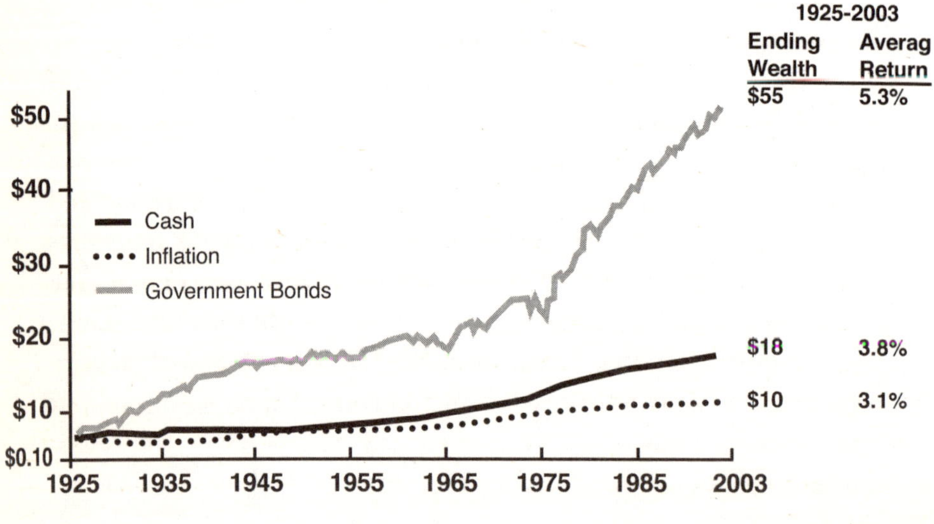

After adjusting for inflation, the real return of bonds (real return means that the return has been adjusted to account for the effect of inflation) has historically been about 3.5 percent. If we include the effect of taxes (even with a 401k or traditional IRA), taxes must be paid eventually), the real return of fixed-income investments hovers around one percent. Allow me to give you an example.

If you were to go out and purchase a five-year CD that paid a nice tidy rate of return of five percent, what would you be left with after inflation and taxes? Currently, inflation is running about three percent. (By the way, a spread of about two percent between five-year CD rates and inflation is about right.) For the purposes of our example, let's assume a forty percent marginal tax bracket. (This may seem high, but when you factor in Federal taxes, State taxes and sales tax, it's not.) The CD you bought is going to pay the promised return of five percent per year. From that five percent return, a portion must immediately be subtracted for taxes in a regular investment account. In this example, we've assumed a forty percent marginal tax rate, so from the five percent we're earning, two percent must be subtracted to satisfy the taxman. This leaves you with an after-tax return of three percent, but inflation is currently running at three percent in this example. Your net return ends up being zero.

A properly diversified bond portfolio would do better than that. As I mentioned above, it could be expected to produce about one percent per year after inflation and taxes over the long term. Either way, the result is basically the same. Fixed-income provides an illusion of safety that can be dangerous to a long-term retirement plan. If you're healthy and under sixty-five years of age or if you're married and under seventy years of age, then you, statistically at least, can expect your spouse or yourself to live for quite some time. If you're going to be around for a long time, then it's only common sense to design your investment plan for the long term.

You may be thinking that the picture would be better in a tax-deferred account, like a 401k or an IRA. You're right. It's better, just not by a whole lot. I won't bore you with the calculations, because there's no reason for you to want to know how to do them, but if we use the same example as above in a tax-deferred account, we come out with a real return of 1.15 percent. That's a heck of a lot better than zero, but in the way that light cigarettes are better for you than regular cigarettes.

Fixed-income investments will safely store the purchasing power of your money, but that's about it. They simply can't be counted on to deliver, by themselves, the type of real return that will provide your family with a lifetime of safety and comfort.

I've been working with investors long enough to know that most of you aren't completely sold on this concept. The vast majority of Americans are still clinging to the misconception that bonds can offer safety. You're remembering the high interest rates of the late '70s and early '80s and thinking *if only*. The purpose of this text is not to show you how to retire with bonds—I simply don't believe that's possible for most Americans. I'll remind you again that the purpose of this book is to show you how to have financial peace of mind. Bonds are an important part of your optimal portfolio, but they're only a part. They have a role to play and that's it. If you rely on bonds to fund the preponderance of your retirement needs, you'll fail. I don't say you *might* fail, I say you *will* fail. I'll only make one guarantee about investing in this book and here it is: if you base your retirement plan 100 percent on fixed income, your plan will fail. The great pension plans know this is true. To them, bonds are simply one of the five asset classes with a role to play. Please try to accept and understand that this is true.

For those of you who still stubbornly think that high interest rates would make bonds more attractive, I'll give you one more example. Let's use that same example we used before; we'll simply change the interest rate to ten percent.

If you were to buy a five-year CD paying ten percent, what would you have left after taxes and inflation? Historically, the five-year CD rate tends to be two to three percent higher than the current inflation rate. Banks earn their profits on what the industry calls "interest rate spreads." In plain English: banks make most of their money from the difference between what they're paying for CDs and what they're charging for loans and mortgages. Banks aren't about to let inflation eat away at their profits of course, so in addition to the interest rate spread, there's an inflation spread. Over the long term, the inflation spread on five-year CDs tends to be two to three percent. In other words, if the five-year CD rate is ten percent, then inflation must be running around seven percent to eight percent. To be conservative, let's assume that it's the lower of the two or seven percent for this example. Your real return (your interest after adjusting for inflation), would be ten percent minus seven percent, or three percent. How much tax would you owe? If we assume the same forty percent tax bracket as above, then you'd owe forty percent of the ten percent return, or four percent. Your total after-tax, after-inflation return, is negative one percent. If we'd performed this calculation using eight percent as the inflation rate instead of seven percent, the net return would've turned out even less favorably, at negative two percent.

You can calculate all the examples you want on your own, but the result will always be the same. Our tax system punishes fixed-income investors. The higher the interest rate, the worse your after-tax real return ends up being. In a tax-differed registered account, the damage isn't as bad, because of the effect of the tax-free compounding, but your real return on that same investment would still look pretty dismal.

This is a tough concept for most people to swallow. As an investment professional, it still took me years to fully grasp the illusion of safety that fixed-income investments provide. At its core, however, there's a perfectly logical reason for this and I'm going to try to share that with you through a story I call "the owner and the loaner."

The Owner and the Loaner

Sheila and Mike were high-school students. They were brother and sister, and their parents didn't have much money, so they knew that if they wanted to attend college, they'd need to pay for most of it themselves. As the school year came to a close, they began the annual summer job search. The competition for summer jobs in their small town was always fierce and with the start of the summer break only weeks away, neither one of them had found a job.

One day, Sheila approached Mike with an idea. She explained to him that the frozen yogurt stand by the beach was for sale. The asking price was $11,000, which was more than either of them could afford, but they decided to meet with the current owner anyway. The frozen yogurt stand was owned by a kindly old man named Mr. Cohn. They both knew him and had both bought frozen yogurt there countless times. Mr. Cohn met them at the stand and began to explain his business to them. He backed up everything he said with a copy of his financial books. They liked what they heard. It seemed the stand did well enough that Mr. Cohn was able to hire a couple of summer students to run the stand for him every summer and there was usually a profit of around $10,000 left over for him when the season ended.

After meeting with Mr. Cohn, Sheila was very excited. She told Mike that they ought to cash out the money they'd saved for college and invest it in the stand. She reasoned to her brother that if they were to buy the stand, there'd be no need to hire the summer students. They could run the stand themselves. After looking at Mr. Cohn's books, Sheila figured that they could afford to pay themselves a fair wage and if they were careful, they should be able to afford to repay their college savings plan as well. Mike thought it over. He liked the idea of working with his sister for the summer and he loved the idea of working near the beach, but he'd been working and saving for three summers to build his college fund and he just didn't feel comfortable risking it. He told this to his sister. She considered the matter carefully, then made him an offer. If he'd loan her $5,000 from his college fund, she'd guarantee him $5,500 at the end of the summer. Mike trusted his sister, but he was still a little leery. He wasn't comfortable with the thought of losing money. Sheila knew how Mike felt, so she improved her offer. She told him that she'd put up the frozen yogurt stand as collateral. If she couldn't repay the loan for some reason, he'd have the frozen yogurt stand, worth $11,000, as security. Mike considered the offer and agreed. After all, he trusted Sheila, and with the entire stand as collateral, he knew his money was safe. Safety was important to Mike.

Later that day, Sheila went to see Mr. Cohn at the yogurt stand. After some spirited negotiating, he agreed to sell her the stand for $10,000. Sheila used the $5,000 she had in her own university account, along with the $5,000 she'd borrowed from her brother, to close the deal.

They were in business! Sheila and Mike had the summer of their lives. They both loved working near the beach and they both enjoyed their jobs. When the summer finally came to an end, it was time to close the yogurt stand for the season. After tidying up, Sheila gave Mike a cheque for the $5,500 she'd promised him. As Mike was picking up the cheque, he noticed a second cheque for $4,500. "Where did that come from?" Mike asked. "That's my profit for the summer," Sheila explained to Mike. Mike was glad that he'd played it safe. After all, he had his $5,000 back plus $500 in interest, while Sheila had apparently only received $4,500 from her original investment of $5,000. He said as much to Sheila. Sheila looked surprised. "I may not have as much money in the bank as you do this year," she said. "But next year I'll still own the yogurt stand and I won't have any loans to pay back." Mike's mouth dropped open in surprise. For the first time in his life, he understood the difference between the owner and the loaner.

* * *

I realize this story is more than a little simplistic, but I hope it makes the point all the same. Mike felt that he was playing it safe and that Sheila was taking all the risk. Was he right? Remember our definition of risk. Risk is the chance that we'll fail to achieve our goals. The goal that Mike and Sheila both shared was to save enough money to attend a good college. In order to achieve his goal, Mike still needs to find a job and save money every summer until he's finished college—a tall order. Sheila, on the other hand, owns a business that will supply her with profits every summer. Sheila has guaranteed herself a job as well as an annual income; she's reduced her risk and achieved her goal. Mike has a bit more money in the bank than he did at the beginning of the summer, but his risk is still the same and his studies are still unfunded.

In the capitalist system—and make no mistake, you live and work in a capitalist country—the owners will always come out ahead of the loaners. They have to; it can work no other way. Do you think a bank would offer to pay you five percent on a CD, if they didn't know they were going to make more than that when they loaned out your money? Of course they wouldn't. Smart owners only borrow money if they're darn sure they can put it to better use. I don't want to turn this book into Economics 101, but you need to understand and believe this. Over the long-term, owners have to make more money than lenders for two reasons. Firstly, businesses wouldn't borrow money unless they were confident they could make a profit. Secondly, and much more importantly, if owners don't make more money than lenders over the long-term, then they simply can't pay the lenders back.

Stop and think about this for a moment, because it's the backbone of the free market economy. It's not unlikely that lenders will make more than owners—it's impossible. If the lenders were to make more than the owners, then the owners simply wouldn't be able to afford to repay the lenders. The great pension plans understand this principle. For that matter, every well-run business in

North America understands this principle. Do you?

I'm not saying this to talk you out of owning fixed-income investments. On the contrary, I insist that you *do* own them. I just want to be certain that you own them for the right reasons. Safety isn't one of those reasons. The only thing a retirement portfolio made up of 100 percent fixed-income guarantees you, is failure. There's only one reason you should own bonds and that's for asset allocation. Fixed-income is one of the pillars of asset allocation. When other asset classes are dropping, your fixed-income asset class will be going up in value and protecting you from volatility. When a recession causes equity prices to drop, there's an excellent chance that the profits from your rising fixed-income investments can be used to scoop up good companies at bargain prices.

Fixed-income has an important role to play in the construction of your optimum portfolio, just make sure you understand that too much of a good thing can be deadly.

Now that you have a better understanding of the advantages and disadvantages of fixed-income, it's time to learn more about the different types. The fixed-income asset class is made up of five subcategories:

1. government bonds
2. CDs
3. corporate bonds
4. preferred shares
5. foreign bonds

Let's take a brief look at each type.

Government Securities

For Americans reading this book, the main type of government security to consider is, of course, from the US government. US treasury's bonds are among the strongest in the world. Because the government controls the tax rates and because it can literally print money if necessary, there's no chance of a default by the federal government, however US treasury's bonds generally yield the lowest return on investment, because of their perceived safety. Typically treasuries are taxable at the federal level, but exempt from state tax. US treasuries that mature within one year are usually referred to as "bills," those that are longer than one year, but shorter than ten are known as "notes," and those longer than ten year as "bonds." While interesting this is a perfect example of the type of detail that you don't really need to know about. For the remainder of this book, I'll be using the terms treasury, note, bond, and fixed income interchangeably.

Federal agencies can also issue bonds. These are backed by the full faith and credit of the US government, and should for our purposes be treated the same as treasury securities. States, cities, and counties also issue bonds. These bonds are commonly called "Muni's." Municipal bonds are generally good quality. Municipalities have control over the local tax rate; if push comes to shove, a municipality can always raise taxes in order to meet its responsibilities. The chance of default, while still remote, is higher for municipal bonds than for US treasury's. As a result, Municipal bonds generally feature additional tax incentives and/or higher yields.

Certificates of Deposit

Certificates of Deposit, CDs, can serve a useful purpose in your financial life. If you have a lump sum of cash and need to park it for a short period of time, CDs will provide certainty and generally pay a better return than a bank account. That's really about all they're good for. Most of the perceived value that CDs offer is an illusion.

When you buy a CD, the value of your investment will always show on your statement as the purchase price plus the interest you've earned. CDs never drop in value; instead they slowly gain in value month after month as the interest compounds. Because CDs can never drop in value, the public perceives them as having no risk. If you've been following this book, however, you know that this isn't really true. CDs are still exposed to the same inflation risk, interest rate risk and currency risk that a bond would be exposed to. CDs can never drop in value for one simple reason—you can't sell them. If you buy a government bond and hold it to maturity, the net result is the same: you'll receive your principal back plus interest at maturity. The difference between goverment treasury's and CDs, lies principally in the fact that government issues are liquid.

Consider this example: Let's say you made two investments. The first investment is $100,000 placed in a five-year CD, paying six percent semi-annually. The second investment is a $100,000 government bond, also paying six percent semi-annually.

The CD will always show on your statement as being worth exactly $100,000 and twice per year, it'll pay $3,000 in interest for a total of $6,000 per year (or six percent). The government bond will also pay $3,000 twice a year. The difference is that you can easily sell a government bond—it's liquid. This means that instead of $100,000, your statement will show the price you could sell the bond for. If you buy the bond and hold it to maturity, there's no difference between it and the CD. The only reason the CD's price stays the same on your statement is because you can't sell it. You know what a bond costs when you buy it and you know what you'll receive when it matures. This is exactly the same as a CD. The liquidity of the bond is an extra feature. Don't make the mistake of thinking that a bond is riskier than a CD because the price can change. The change in price is simply an example of temporary price volatility. One month the price of the bond might be up, the next it might be down. It's just temporary. You know what the bond will mature for.

You must avoid confusing temporary price volatility (which most people perceive as risk) with actual risk (the chance that you'll fail to reach your goal). How much money you're going to make over the life of the investment is the key consideration.

When constructing your asset allocation, consider CDs and government bonds to be one and the same (fixed-income); select that which best fits your portfolio.

There's one more point I'd like to make on the subject of CDs.

Much is made of the FDIC (Federal Deposit Insurance Corporation) coverage that protects the money you invest in a CD. Deposits of up to $100,000 are insured against the default of the issuing bank, trust company or deposit broker. It's nice that CDs are protected—it gives people confidence and eliminates worry—but consider who's ultimately behind the FDIC guarantee: the federal government. Treasury securities and federal agency bonds offer the unconditional guarantee of the US Government, regardless of the amount invested. Make the choice based on length and yield. Both guarantees are fine.

Corporate Bonds

In the fixed-income asset class, corporate bonds generally provide the highest returns. Historically, corporate bonds have yielded roughly an extra half percent per year, compared with federal government securities. That may not seem like much, but when you remember that we're also reducing risk by diversifying, it's a pretty good deal.

When considering a corporate bond, one of the most important factors to look at is the company's ability to repay its debt. This may seem difficult, but thanks to bond rating agencies, it's actually very simple. The three main bond rating agencies are Standard & Poor's, Moodies and Fitch. These companies specialize in assessing the ability of companies, and even governments, to repay debt.

Bonds are rated according to the following system.

AAA – Highest credit quality
AA
A
BBB
BB
B
CCC
CC

C
D – Lowest credit quality

Bond rating agencies will commonly add a + or a - sign to a given rating, to indicate if it's a little better or worse than most bonds carrying that rating. A bond rated "A+" is slightly better than the average "A" rated bond. Likewise, a bond rated "A-" is still deserving of an "A" rating, but its credit quality is slightly less than that of the average "A" rated bond. As a general rule, bonds rated at or above the BBB level are considered "investment grade." This means that they're good quality bonds with a relatively small chance of default. As the credit rating improves, the chance of default goes down. Conservative investors, like pension funds and like us, won't even consider investing in any bond that's not rated investment grade.

So why wouldn't everyone simply use "AAA" rated bonds? As you probably know, the yields that bonds pay tend to increase as the credit quality drops. In other words, as the risk increases, so does the return. Does the increased return justify owning corporate bonds? Of course it does. On average, the owners of investment grade corporate bonds earn one half percent more per year than the owners of Government bonds. Due to the magic of compound interest, that half percent translates into an overall increase in return of about ten percent over a twenty-year period. As my grandmother likes to say, mind the pennies and the dollars will take care of themselves.

Preferred Shares

Unlike bonds, which can be issued by either corporations or governments, preferred shares can only be issued by corporations. If you're ever confused about whether you own a bond or a preferred share, all you need to do is look at the price. Bonds are always issued in denominations of $100. Preferred shares, on the other hand, are almost always issued in denominations of $25. They're set up this way to eliminate confusion on the part of investors. It's been my experience, however, that there's still plenty of confusion to go around.

Like a corporate bond, a preferred share is a debt obligation of a company. The price of a company's stock has nothing to do with the preferred shares. If the company does well and its stock goes up, that's great, but there's no benefit to preferred shareholders. What a preferred shareholder is entitled to is a steady stream of income. Regardless of increases or decreases in a company's profits, a preferred shareholder will still receive the same income. Based on what I've said so far, you may be wondering what the difference between a preferred share and a bond is. That's a good question. So far, they're basically the same. In fact, there are only two main differences between bonds and preferred shares.

The first difference is that preferred shareholders are paid dividends, not interest. This is important because of preferential tax treatment of dividends. Currently the maximum federal tax rate on dividend income is fifteen percent, compared with thirty-eight percent on interest and employment income. In other words, you'll pay about half as much tax on dividend income than you will on interest income received from a bond or CD.

If you're paying a large amount of tax, preferred shares can provide some significant advantages. It's important to note, however, that there's absolutely no advantage from receiving dividend income in a tax-deferred account, such as a 401k or an IRA. For this reason, you'd never want to purchase a preferred share in any of the nine types of Individual Retirement Accounts.

The second difference is that bonds are paid before preferred shares if a company has serious financial difficulty. This may seem important, but it's really not. Conservative investors, like us, simply don't invest with companies that may not be able to repay us.

The credit quality of preferred shares is ranked by the same large rating agencies that cover bonds. The rating scale for preferred shares is simpler than the one used for bonds.

P1 – Highest credit quality

P2 – Superior credit quality
P3 – Adequate credit quality, considered investment grade
P4 – Below average
P5 – Lowest credit quality

Each rating starts with a "P," so you always know that it refers to a preferred share. As with bonds, the scale starts with the highest credit quality and moves down. "P1" is the highest rated preferred share and "P5" is the lowest rated. Rating agencies will also frequently use the suffixes "high" and "low" to indicate that an issuer is above or slightly below average. "P2 high" is a slightly better rating than "P2."

When it comes to building your personal pension plan, only preferred shares rated "P1" or "P2" are appropriate. Remember, conservative investors only invest money with good quality companies.

Foreign Bonds

Simply put, a foreign bond is any bond not issued in the United States. The rating system for foreign bonds is identical to the rating system for domestic bonds. The most common question I hear about foreign bonds is, "Why do I want to own them?" In order to answer that question, I ask you to think back to the five risks. Four of those risks are interest rate risk, inflation risk, currency risk and market risk. All of these risks can be reduced and eliminated within a properly designed plan, and foreign bonds have an important role to play.

Foreign bonds are purchased in the currency of the issuing country. Canadian bonds would be purchased in Canadian dollars and European bonds would be purchased in euros. In the investment community, these types of bonds are commonly referred to as Canuk and Euro bonds. The interest on these bonds is paid in the currency of the issuing country and, when they eventually mature, the principal is repaid in the same manner.

How does this help us? Simple. By investing in the bonds of

foreign countries, we're helping to diversify away four out of the five big risks. The interest rate cycle in Europe, Asia or even Australia is different from the cycle in the United States. When rates are going up in one country, they may be going down in another. The same holds true of inflation rates and currency values. Now, I want you to think about this carefully and then answer the following question: If an investment portfolio is properly diversified, how would it be affected by a change in exchange rates?

The answer to this question may seem a tad simple, but there's good reason for that. You already know what it is! As discussed in Chapter 4, a properly diversified portfolio is relatively unaffected by exchange rates. Any gain or drop in the currency of one country, should be more or less offset by a corresponding move in the value of the world's other currencies. Currency exchange is a zero-sum game. Taken as a group, the currencies of the world change in value only by inflation or, in rare cases, deflation.

The great pension fund managers understand the value and importance of foreign bonds. They realize that as part of a properly balanced portfolio, foreign bonds help reduce and eliminate four of the five big risks: currency, inflation, interest rate and market risk.

Asset Allocation and Equities

This is by far the most difficult section of the book for me to write. People devote their entire lives to becoming experts on the equity markets. There are thousands of books available on the topic and you can even get a Master's degree on the subject if you want. When there's that much information available on a single topic, it becomes difficult to tune out the noise (a problem many of you will understand). The purpose of this book is not to teach you how to be an expert stock picker. My purpose, in fact sometimes I feel it's my calling in life, is to show you how to build a pension that will protect both your family and yourself. You don't need to be an expert in stocks to build such a plan. In fact, I think it would hold you back. For this reason, I'm not going to spend any time trying to teach you how to pick the best stocks or equity mutual funds. If you just want to pick "the best" equity investments, there are literally hundreds of books on the shelves of your local bookstore that can show you the current "hot system."

Any system is better than no system. A bad system is better than no system. But I have two questions to ask you. Why on earth would anyone entrust their family's security to a bad system? And perhaps more importantly, if all the hundreds of investment systems and strategies you see on the news, in magazines and in books, work so well, then why aren't any pension funds using them? You won't find any pension funds doing these things, because there's a better way. It's as simple as that.

I don't mean to sound like a broken record, but I have to make sure you're on board with this. There's no magic bullet. I'll admit that your specific choice of equity investments does have a role to play in the success of your plan. But it has nowhere near the importance that the financial media would try to portray. What difference does it make to a pension plan if the markets were up fifty points today or down fifty points? None. We need to learn to ignore the noise. And it's almost all noise.

So if none of that's important, what is? When it comes to building the equity portion of a pension fund, there are only five points you need to understand.

1. Over the very long term, stocks will always be the highest performing asset class.
2. Over the very long term, stocks are the "safest" asset class.
3. Short-term volatility is not your real risk.
4. You cannot outsmart the equity markets.
5. Rebalancing is the key.

Owners will always beat loaners. This is the fundamental law of the free market economy. Remember, an equity investment isn't just some piece of paper. It represents direct ownership in the company. Over the long term, if companies don't make more than lenders, then the lenders can't be repaid. I know it can seem like an act of faith to accept this, but I assure you this law isn't built on faith. It's built on the fundamental fabric of our country's financial system. It's imperative to your family's long-term financial safety that you ignore the day-to-day noise of the media and accept reality. No matter how wrong it may feel to you—I promise—owners beat loaners.

The graph below compares both the best and worst returns of the equity market over one-, two-, five-, ten-, twenty- and thirty-year periods. In the short term, volatility plays a big part and returns are highly unpredictable, but as we move from short term to long term, the volatility shrinks and returns become increasingly predictable and consistent.

EQUITIES ARE VOLATILE IN THE SHORT-TERM BUT ARE THE SAFEST IN THE LONG-TERM (FIG. 9)

Highest/lowest rate of return for stocks

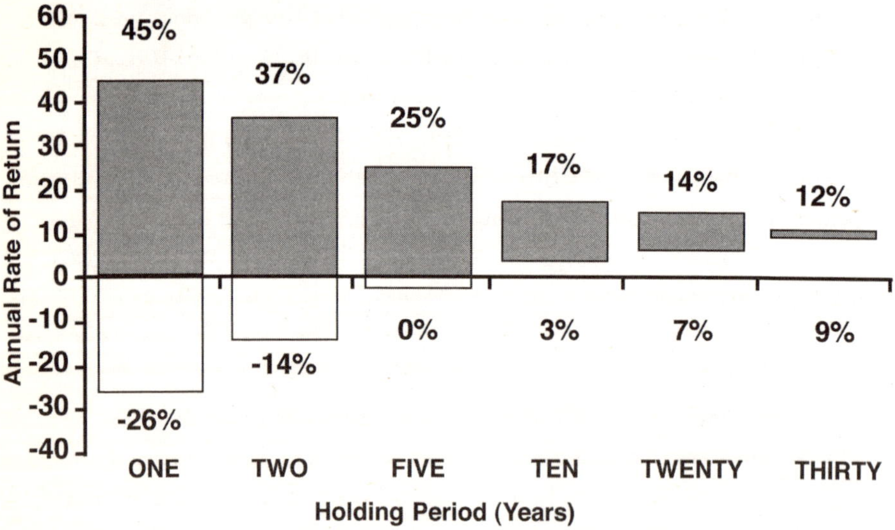

SOURCE: Merrill Lynch Canada
TSE 300 from 1950-2000

Inflation-Proofing Equities

In 1975, the cost of one first-class stamp was ten cents. Today, that same first-class stamp costs thirty-seven cents. Does that bring the risk of inflation a little closer to home? Almost everyone who started saving for retirement in 1975 is still active and healthy today. For that matter, many of the people who *retired* in 1975 are still going strong. But how are their finances doing? If their portfolios were heavy on cash and fixed income, the answer is, badly. Since 1975, the cost of a stamp has increased by 370 percent; the cost of houses, cars, movies and groceries have undergone increases as well.

Remember the five big risks?

1. currency risk
2. interest rate risk
3. inflation risk
4. manager risk
5. market risk

Of the five big risks, the hardest to comprehend, and by far the most devastating, is inflation risk. Inflation is insidious. It eats away at your principal in an almost invisible fashion. But make no mistake, the fact that inflation risk works slowly, doesn't change the devastation it causes. The best analogy I can think of is erosion. It works slowly as well. In fact, we can rarely recognize its effects in our lifetime, but inevitably mountains become hills and boulders become sand under its relentless attack. Inflation represents erosion of not only your savings, but also the financial security and comfort of your family.

The only asset class that's completely inflation proof is equities. They may be volatile in the short term, but over the long term, equities eliminate inflation risk. I'm sure you've heard "stocks are risky" hundreds of times. You may have even said it yourself. I ask you now to open your mind and really think about it. This is important. Used properly, equities provide the only effective way of eliminating the biggest risk to your family's long-term financial security: inflation. Where's the risk in that? Of course the short-term volatility of equities is higher than that of fixed-income and cash. It has to be! The higher short-term volatility is the cost of the higher long-term returns and the inbuilt inflation protection equities provide. I ask you again, which is really safer? The often bumpy path of equities, which will have to travel through hills and valleys on the way to completely eliminating inflation risk, or the smooth, but constantly eroding, path of fixed-income?

As hard as it may be to believe, over the long term, the safest asset class isn't cash and it isn't fixed-income. When all five of the big risks are considered, it's the equity asset class which carries the lowest risk. Over the long term, volatility disappears and risk becomes simply the chance that you'll fail to achieve your goals.

I know this can be a tough pill to swallow, but your portfolio isn't going to get better unless you take your medicine. Every single pension fund in North America utilizes the equity asset class to help manage inflation risk. If you're serious about getting the five big risks out of your plan, you'll need to use the same tools that the great pension fund managers use.

The most intensive study ever undertaken on the subject of investment risk was by Dr. Jeremy Siegel, a professor with the Wharton School of Business. After researching 200 years of interest rate, inflation and stock market data he concluded that, "Although it might appear to be riskier to hold stocks than bonds, precisely the opposite is true: the safest long-term investment for the preservation of purchasing power has clearly been stocks, not bonds."

In my experience, the most common mistake investors make is failing to understand risk. In a properly diversified portfolio, equities help to reduce the overall risk. The common misconception is, of course, that equities increase risk. Hopefully, you're starting to realize that this really isn't the case. Why is the misconception so prevalent? The vast majority of the investing public, including many professionals, confuse volatility with risk. Volatility and risk are both words with negative connotations.

When you think about these two words, you probably experience the same sinking feeling in the pit of your stomach, regardless of which word is used. This is the mistake.

Risk really is a four-letter word. I don't blame anyone for wanting to avoid it. I personally don't take unnecessary risks and I don't think any sane person should. Remember that the first assumption Markowitz makes in modern portfolio theory is that all investors would like to avoid risk whenever possible. For any targeted level of return, there exists a lowest-risk portfolio that will achieve it. Our goal here is to provide a safe, secure pension for yourself and your family. There's no room for unnecessary risk in a safe and secure plan. Let's leave risk to the daredevils.

Volatility, on the other hand, is very different from risk. Volatility is the term used to describe the temporary price swings our markets are always experiencing. Price volatility in the stock markets isn't a bad thing at all. It's simply the result of millions of people all over the world trying to outsmart each other at the same time. The market prices of individual stocks, or of entire indexes, are in a constant state of flux, always moving so that half the people think they're too high and the other half think they're too low. Market prices always have to stay in the middle. It's like a natural law: the weight of all the people who think the market is too low will continuously move the market higher, until it's offset by an equal weight of people who think it's too high. The Dow drops 200 points, it gains 150 points, it all means nothing in the long term—it's just more noise.

All these people who're trying to outsmart each other just don't get it. It can't be done. In the end, they're only outsmarting themselves. But we should be grateful for this, because ultimately, it's the very volatility they create that provides the premium return of equities. If the short-term or even the medium-term prices of equities were predictable, then the returns would be the same as fixed-income. The more unpredictable the short-term prices of equities are, the higher the long-term returns will be. It's really that simple. Volatility is our friend.

But wait a minute. If short-term price volatility is actually good for our returns, why do so many people confuse volatility and risk? Panic. These people don't have a plan in place. I'll never understand how someone could risk the financial future of themselves and their families without a well-designed plan, but the fact remains that it happens everyday. In a pension fund, short-term price volatility is almost irrelevant. When equity prices drop, two or more of the other asset classes usually move upwards. This is what modern portfolio theory is about: reducing and eliminating risks. What is a short-term drop in the stock markets anyway? Think of the five big risks. A drop in the stock market is simply market risk. A properly designed portfolio has control of its market risk through the use of asset allocation. Stock prices periodically drop. It's completely outside our control and frankly, it isn't even all that rare. On average, there's a drop of more than thirty percent in equity prices every five years. If it happens every five years, it's not unexpected! Through asset allocation, we plan for and eliminate market risk. Investors who don't plan for market risk tend to have a slightly different reaction—*panic*. When the unprepared see prices dropping, they panic and sell. When they panic and sell, presto! Volatility becomes risk.

Please allow me to repeat myself. Volatility and risk are not the same thing. Volatility is not the risk, even for the poor souls who panic and sell. What's their risk? The risk these people take is, unfortunately, their own behaviour. Take another look at the chart following; you've seen it before. Over ninety percent of your lifetime investment returns will come from the asset allocation you choose. Think about what that means for a second. Who controls your asset allocation? You do, with your behaviour. You can choose to behave like a lemming and follow the crowd off the next cliff or you can choose to manage your money the way the great pension fund managers do. Ultimately, it's up to you

Fixed-income, real estate and equities all undergo short-term price volatility. For the most part, equities are the most volatile of these three asset classes and fixed-income is the least, but that's

CONTRIBUTIONS TO LIFE-TIME INVESTMENT PERFORMANCE (FIG. 10)

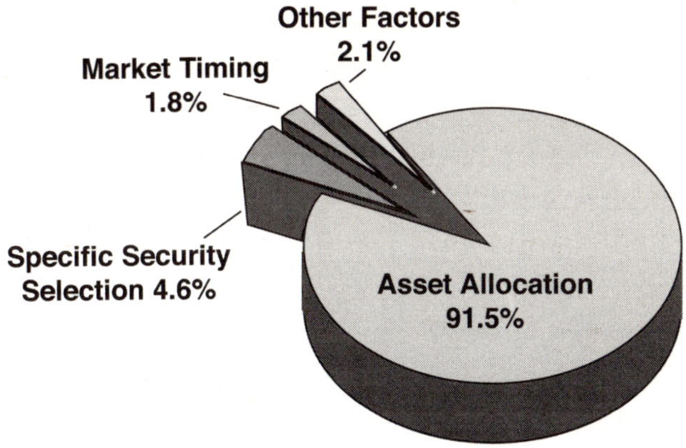

Source: Financial Analysts Journal, May/June 1991, "Determinants of Portfolio Performance II: An update" by Brinson, Singer and Beebower.

not even important. What is important is that the great pension plans not only cruise comfortably though short-term price volatility, they profit from it! The very same factors that will reduce the current price of a plan's equity holdings, will push up the price of at least some of its other asset classes. Do they wait patiently for natural market forces to restore their portfolio to equilibrium? No. Pension funds rebalance their portfolios. When pension funds rebalance, they take a portion of the profits from the stronger performing asset classes and use it to buy more of the temporarily underperforming asset class. In other words, they sell high and buy low.

The great pension funds repeat this process year after year, taking advantage of short-term price volatility to sell high and buy low. One year it may be real estate sold to buy equities, the next it may be equities sold to buy bonds. It doesn't matter. Year after year the process is repeated and the result will always be the same. There's no magic bullet, it doesn't require excessive risk, it doesn't even take very much work. It's just modern portfolio theory and the discipline to stick with your plan.

I'm sure you still have many questions about rebalancing. Not to fear, we'll discuss it in more detail later.

Why Do Equities Work?

As I mentioned earlier, I'm not going to go into great detail on equities in this book. There have been many great books written on the subject and I don't feel the need to repeat someone else's work. Perhaps, more importantly, I just don't think you need to know that much about them. In my opinion, you really only need to grasp three concepts to make effective use of equities.

1. why you need them
2. what they will do for you
3. why they will always work

If you understand these three basic concepts about equities, then you'll truly be prepared to understand how they fit into your private pension fund. Understanding will lead to comfort and confidence. In the end, these things are much more important than charts and research reports.

Remember the owner versus loaner analogy? It highlights the most basic reason why equities will always continue to work for conservative investors. In short, the owner versus loaner analogy teaches us that the average company will always have to generate a higher return from borrowed funds than it's paying to borrow them. If companies can't make higher returns than their cost of borrowing, then they won't borrow. What would be the point? Corporations are in business to make profit. If they can make higher profits by not borrowing, then you can be sure they'll quickly stop borrowing.

There's another reason why the owner must always make more money than the loaner. How is the loaner going to be repaid if the borrower doesn't earn more? Borrowing still more? That won't last for long. The free market system is ruthlessly efficient and very powerful. Companies that borrow money must earn a higher return on that money than they pay in interest. If they don't, they go out of business. How are they going to pay back the loan then?

If a company goes out of business, both the owner and the loaner will lose at least part of their investments. If a company is successful, the owner will always make more than the loaner.

The only advantage that the loaner gets in exchange for accepting what's sure to be an inferior long-term return, is certainty. They can be certain what they're going to make and when they're going to make it. The owner gets the advantage of a higher long-term return, but has to accept some uncertainty, because she can't quite be sure when she'll see her profits.

If you have $100,000 earmarked for the purchase of a cottage in three years, do you want to be an owner or a loaner? A loaner, obviously. The most important consideration is having the $100,000 available when it comes time to buy the cottage and you should be willing to sacrifice potentially higher returns for certainty.

When we're discussing your pension plan, the exact opposite is true. The short-term certainty of fixed-income becomes the long-term risk of failure and the short-term uncertainty of owning great companies becomes the long-term security of inflation-proof returns.

The Real Value of Companies

Much of the perceived risk of owning equities stems from a basic misunderstanding of value. The newspapers, Internet and TV list and discuss the market value of companies. The market value is the price you could get today if you sold. This is important, no doubt about it, but it's more important not to confuse the market value of a company with the *real* value of that same company.

It's not that uncommon to see on the news that the market value of a great company, such as Coca-Cola, has dropped ten or even twenty percent in one day. Don't be fooled. Do you really think the value of Coke's business dropped by twenty percent in a single day? Did twenty percent of its factories disappear? Did people suddenly decide to start drinking twenty percent less cola? Of course they didn't. In fact, the real value of the company didn't change one bit. All that happened is that the price someone is willing to pay to buy a share in the company changed.

There's only one predictor of stock price that consistently and accurately works over time. That predictor is, of course, the value of the company. Over the short term, the market value of the company can move up and down, it can be higher or lower than the real value of the company, but over the long term the market value of any company's stock will tend to follow the real value of the company.

The great pension funds understand this. They invest in high-quality companies that grow their earnings over time. After all, what's the real value of a company? A company's real value is its earnings power.

Over time, the earnings of a good quality company are going to grow in four ways.

1. inflation
2. the growth of the Gross Domestic Product (GDP)
3. retained earnings
4. growth of the business

We've discussed the topic of inflation already. In a good quality company, inflation eventually flows through the prices of the goods or services produced and increases the bottom line by the same amount.

GDP measures the value of the goods or services produced by the nation's economy. GDP growth doesn't include the effects of inflation. A GDP growth rate of two percent for the year effectively means that two percent more business was done in the country than had been done the year before. Any decently run company will find that its sales and earnings automatically increase with the GDP growth rate.

Retained earnings are profits that a company earns, but doesn't pay out to shareholders. Instead, the company keeps these profits and invests them in future growth. Retained earnings may be used to expand existing operations, buy back the company's own shares or buy up the competition. The result is the same—the company's sales and earnings should always increase, in direct proportion to the amount of earnings retained.

The fourth way that a good quality company will grow its earnings is the one you're probably the most familiar with: sales growth. Good companies increase market share, they gain new customers and they get better at what they do. Perhaps the industry as a whole is expanding or new products and services are being brought to the market. Every company starts out by doing a good job of growing its business. What good would inflation, GDP growth and retained earnings do a company that has no sales and profits? The well-run companies of the world continue to grow their business naturally. The day they stop growing their businesses, is the day they stop being well run.

The market prices of equities won't go up every year; this is called volatility and it's to be expected. The real value of good quality companies does go up almost every year however, and it's not just to be expected, it's practically a law of nature. Inflation, GDP growth and retained earnings work together to grow the real value of good companies in good times and bad.

Let's look at how the earnings break down at a typical bank as an example. The typical bank stock trades at roughly eleven times earnings as I write this. What this means is that for every dollar you invest, the bank will earn nine cents in profit. If you were to invest $10,000 in the typical bank stock, the bank would earn about $909 in profit that year based on your capital.

What do they do with these profits? The typical bank pays out roughly thirty-five percent of all profits it earns in the form of dividends to the shareholders. If you've invested $10,000, then you'll receive a dividend for thirty-five percent of the $909 profit your investment earned.

Three hundred and eighteen dollars would be paid to you; this amounts to a return of 3.18 percent on your original investment of $10,000. The bank keeps the other $591 it earned as retained earnings. If the market price of the bank's shares seems low compared to its real value, then the bank might use the retained earnings to buy back its own shares, directly increasing your share of the profits. The company might use the retained earnings to open new branches or buy up smaller competitors. Ultimately, it doesn't matter to you, because the result is the same; sales, revenue and of course the bank's profits will increase proportionately.

The second year you own the typical bank stock, the picture changes quite a bit. The profits used to be $900 but now they've grown by 6 percent, due to the investment of the retained earnings. Where the bank earned $900 the year before, it's now earning $954. But wait, what about the effect of inflation and GDP growth? On average, inflation in America runs at a healthy 2.5 percent and GDP growth averages about three percent annually. Recall that these should automatically flow to the bottom line of a well-run company. Your $954 in earnings has increased by a further 5.5 percent to a total of $1,006.

Last year, you received a dividend of $318 for your ownership in the typical bank. Will you receive the same this year? Likely not. Remember that the typical bank pays out thirty-five percent of its profits in the form of a dividend. The bank's profits have now increased to $1,006. The dividend will increase accordingly to $352. The bank will keep the other sixty-five percent of the profit as retained earnings of $654. What will it do with the retained earnings? It'll do the same thing it did last year; buy back shares, expand or buy up smaller banks.

The cycle continues perpetually.

The third year you own the typical bank stock in this example, it would be earning $1,122 and you'd be paid a dividend of $393.

This isn't the exception, it's the rule. Good quality companies grow their earnings and dividends consistently. The stock price might be up or it might be down. We can't control it and, in the short term, we can't predict it, but we do know one thing: over the long term, the market value (stock price) of a company will follow its earnings.

If we take this example forward ten years, we'll find that the typical bank has increased its earnings and dividends by an average of 11.1 percent per year. In the short term, stock prices are inherently unpredictable, but I think you can see that if dividends and profits grow by an average of eleven percent per year, the real value of the company will grow as well and the stock price will eventually follow.

Interestingly enough, on a historical basis, the stock market as a whole has seen average growth of about 11.5 percent per year. Is this a coincidence? I hope I just showed you that it's not. Equities are the driving force behind the success of the great pension funds. In the short term they're volatile, but great money managers know that short-term volatility is not long-term risk. In the long term, equities help control inflation risk, and because owners beat loaners, they actually increase the long-term safety of an investment portfolio.

Asset Allocation and Real Estate

Because most of you will have experienced homeownership at some point in your lives, real estate is going to be one of the simplest asset classes for me to explain. There are two schools of thought when it comes to considering real estate as an asset class. One school of thought believes that the value of your home and any other real estate you own, such as a cottage, should be included in your asset allocation. The second position, and the one which I take, is that you have to live somewhere. If you didn't own a home, you'd be paying rent and therefore your home should not be included in your overall asset allocation. As far as I'm concerned, your home is part of your lifestyle. Most people choose to live where they do because of family and lifestyle considerations, not because of investment considerations. I also feel that a secure retirement would include the option of remaining in your home as long as you want and are able to. The final reason I feel this way, is that the vast majority of homes don't produce any type of cash flow. As you'll see, the stream of cash flow that investment real estate produces is one of the primary features that differentiate it from the other asset classes. In this book, we won't include your family home when determining your asset allocation.

Real estate lowers the overall risk of your investment portfolio in several ways. Similarly to equities, the real estate asset class helps to reduce inflation risk. If you've ever rented an apartment or house, then you're well aware that landlords will pass inflation directly on to tenants. Most commercial leases for office space or retail space are automatically adjusted for inflation on an annual basis. When you've rented, do you ever remember your rent going down?

The real estate asset class also helps eliminate interest rate risk and market risk. The steady stream of income that real estate investments are known for and the market value of the property itself, aren't affected by the same short-term influences and volatility as the equity and fixed-income markets are. The technical term to describe this is correlation. Investment real estate is not strongly correlated to the returns of the equity markets. In fact, the steady income stream often causes the market value of investment real estate to be pushed higher during drops in the equity markets. Think back to the largest drops in the stock market that took place during your lifetime: the tech bubble in 2000, the crash of 1987, the nifty-fifty fiasco of the early 1970s. Real estate invariably shines during these times as frantic investors chase the consistent income streams of real estate.

One of the great features of the real estate asset class is that it's much easier for most investors to hold during bad times than equity. What most real estate investors are concerned about is the income stream. As long as the income stream is stable, they're happy and when it increases, they're even happier. For the most part, real estate investors don't concern themselves with the current resale value of their property. What would be the point? If they want to keep receiving the income (and trust me they do), then they can't sell the property.

When did you last have your home appraised? Unless you're planning to sell, it probably wasn't very recently. Most of us are interested to hear what the neighbor's house sold for and we may even go so far as to make mental comparisons with our own property, but we usually draw the line there. Because we live in our homes and plan to continue doing so, we don't get too excited or too despondent when we think our homes have changed in value. This is a healthy attitude and I applaud it. In fact, I wish we were capable of looking at our entire investment portfolio in the same light. The reason most of us aren't able to look at equities that way is that we're constantly barraged by market price updates (in other words, short-term price volatility). One of the great strengths of investment real estate is that, just like your house, it's psychologically immune to short-term price volatility.

Now I'm not suggesting you rush out to purchase the nearest four-plex in your neighborhood. Direct ownership of an investment property might make sense for those of you with handyman skills and free time on your hands, but for most of us, it's not the ideal solution.

So what is the ideal solution? For the most part, the great pension funds don't manage investment properties directly. They own shopping malls, office buildings and apartment buildings, but they don't manage them themselves. The pensions use professional real estate managers to make sure they get the most from their investments, without having to perform all the time-consuming tasks associated with real estate investment. Someone has to collect the rent cheques, keep the buildings maintained and fill vacancies whenever they open up. Pension managers certainly aren't going to waste their own time moonlighting in property management and, fortunately, you don't have to either.

Real estate investment trusts (REITs) are a great solution for most private investors. A REIT can invest anywhere in the country and it can even have a small percentage of its assets in other countries. The large size of most REITs allows them to diversify the locations of their properties, as well as the types of properties they invest in. This geographic and business diversification keeps the cash flow of REITs remarkably consistent throughout different economic cycles.

There are REITs that invest in all sorts of different investment properties, but the most common are:

- office buildings
- shopping malls
- apartment buildings
- hotels
- retirement homes

The vast majority of pensions tend to invest primarily in apartment buildings, office buildings and shopping malls. The consistency and dependability of these three types of real estate is superior to that of hotels and retirement homes. Hotels are extremely dependent on the health of the economy and retirement homes always run the risk of being derailed by a sudden shift in government policy. Remember that the reason we include real estate investments in our asset allocation is to lower our overall risk level. In order to help us to accomplish this, the real estate we invest in must be reliable and consistent enough to provide a stable income stream during bad times.

The main disadvantage of REITs is that they trade on the stock market. Because they trade on the market, REITs can suffer from the same short-term price volatility as equities. What you need to remember is that a REIT is just a group of individual properties, the same as your home. Admittedly REITs are much, much larger, but that doesn't matter. Like your home, the real value of the properties contained within an REIT changes very infrequently. Any short-term price volatility you see is just noise. It may even be a great opportunity to rebalance and take profits.

The important features to look for in any REIT are reliability and yield. You want to choose a good quality REIT that enjoys a high dividend and consistently increasing rents. This isn't something you need to do for yourself. A good investment advisor can help you to select the REITs that make the most sense for you. Several pension funds have even put their own real estate holdings in REIT format and opened them to the public. This allows them to reduce their own share of the management expenses, while at the same time helping the general public build their own plans.

When making a real estate investment, most pension funds look for a return on their capital that's roughly 4.5 percent higher than the current yield of the a thirty-year Government treasury bond. If the thirty-year government bond is yielding six percent, you should be looking for a yield of at least 10.5 percent in your real estate investments. Depending on the current environment, you may be able to do better than this, or you may have to settle for a little worse. The important thing to remember is that real estate is just another asset class. Occasionally, it may hold back your returns, but in a stock market correction, it can save your bacon.

Whether you have the time to manage an investment property yourself or you choose the professional management of an REIT, by including real estate in your investment portfolio, you'll be helping control interest rate risk and inflation risk, and you'll be further diversifying away the market risk and manager risk in your investment portfolio. Pension managers understand this and that's why you'll find real estate playing an important role in every great pension fund.

Absolute Return Investments and Asset Allocation

Absolute return investments are designed to reach a targeted annual return, regardless of movement in the stock markets or bond markets. They're generally immune to movements in interest rates and inflation. There are two separate categories of absolute return investments: real return bonds and absolute return funds.

The US Treasury first started issuing real return bonds in 1997, called Treasury Inflation Protected Securities, or TIPS. Some municipal governments and corporations now issue real return bonds as well. Real return bonds have both their principal and interest payments indexed to the Consumer Price Index (CPI). In a nutshell, this means that both the money you invest and the interest on that money are increased by this amount of inflation every year.

If you were to invest $10,000 in a regular government bond with an interest rate of four percent per year, how much interest would you receive? Well, you'd receive four percent of $10,000 or $400. Straight forward enough. A real return bond works in the same way, but with one twist. At the end of every year, the principal amount of your investment and your interest payment are increased by the amount of inflation. If inflation was three percent that year, then your original investment of $10,000 would be increased to $10,300 (this is the new maturity value of your bond) and the interest payment would go from $400 to $412. Real return bonds are very much an absolute return investment. After adjusting for inflation, the total return you earn will be stable for the life of the bond. Regular bonds, on the other hand, will fluctuate with market forces. If interest rates or inflation increase, the value of traditional bonds will generally decline. Real return bonds, however, would likely be among the strongest performers in your portfolio under these same market conditions. Proper diversification is all about balance, and by virtue of their inbuilt inflation protection, real return bonds are a key component of every properly balanced pension fund.

The second type of absolute return investment is absolute return funds. In the financial world, absolute return funds are commonly referred to as "market neutral hedge funds." They're described as market neutral, because their strategies act to remove the broad movements of the equity and bond markets from their returns. The managers of these funds work to capture and profit from price inefficiencies in the financial markets. The details of these strategies are often complex and, as such, are beyond the scope of this text, but the end result is a remarkably consistent stream of returns in most market environments.

I know this sounds complex and, to some of you, it probably sounds risky. Please allow me to assure you that there's no need for concern. Putting all the fancy terminology aside, absolute return funds are, at their core, simple. Regular mutual funds invest in some combination of stocks and bonds and make a profit only if these investments increase in value. If markets decline, mutual funds will almost always decline as well. They're long-term investments and they're volatile. Absolute return funds couldn't be more different. Volatility is much lower, often eighty to ninety percent lower, in fact. The returns are also much more consistent, hence their inclusion in the absolute return asset class. Stock markets, interest rates, inflation—these things don't have nearly the effect on absolute return funds as they do on mutual funds. Is it any wonder that the great pension funds have been using the absolute return asset class for decades?

Hopefully, you remember that one of the primary benefits of modern portfolio theory is that it allows us to construct an investment portfolio with a greater level of return for a given level of risk than any of the individual components could possibly have on their own. Absolute return investments have no statistically significant correlation to any of the other four asset classes—cash, fixed-income, equities or real estate. Because of the way absolute return investments march to the beat of their own distinct drum, they can increase the returns of your portfolio while decreasing your overall risk. Now that's what I call a neat trick!

If you've been paying attention, right now you may be thinking, "Don't the other four asset classes do this as well?" The answer is that all five asset classes contribute to increasing returns while lowering the risk of a portfolio below the level that any one of the classes, by itself, would undergo. The absolute return asset class is nonetheless special, as it's the only asset class that doesn't have a significant correlation with anything else. Absolute returns will give you the most bang for your buck when it comes to reducing both the volatility and the risk of your portfolio.

Every pension fund that I'm aware of uses absolute return investments to cut short-term volatility and boost long-term returns. If you haven't heard of this asset class, you're not alone. The high minimum investments required have kept absolute return investments out of retail investors' reach until relatively recently. Even today, many of the best managers still require minimum investments of $1, $5 or even $10 million.

I realize that most of you reading this book don't have that kind of money and, even if you did, you'd still need to allocate money to the other four asset classes. The great pension funds obviously don't have this problem. Their huge sizes have always allowed them to benefit from access to the highest quality managers, regardless of the minimum required investment.

This lack of access has long been one of the missing pieces in the pension puzzle for regular American investors. Without the contribution of absolute returns, it's quite simply impossible to duplicate the superior performance, safety and comfort provided by the large pension plans. Fortunately, this problem has been solved in recent years.

What has changed to allow average Americans access to absolute returns? The advent of the "fund of funds" concept. A fund of funds is basically a highly developed mutual fund, whose purpose is to group individual investors' money together, in order to meet the high minimums set by the most highly skilled absolute return managers. A fund of funds has the additional advantage of a senior professional manager, who'll ensure that the individual absolute return investments selected, continue to avoid positive correlation with each other and the other four asset classes. This extra layer of management can add to the overall administrative costs, but given the obvious benefits—lower short-term volatility and higher long-term returns—I believe them to be a bargain. Based on your goals and the size of your investment portfolio, your investment advisor can help you determine whether the fund of funds route or direct ownership of individual absolute return investments is best for you.

Conclusion

Congratulations! You now understand the basics of the five major asset classes. A note of caution: after learning about the five classes, you may have a favorite or favorites. There's always a temptation to leave one or two of the asset classes out of your portfolio. Cash is almost certainly going to be the worst-performing asset in your portfolio, so why include it? You're going to be more comfortable with some asset classes than with others. It's only human nature. However, it's imperative that you fight the urge to leave any out of your personal retirement plan. The greatest pension managers in the world have been working with modern portfolio theory for over fifty years. They've tinkered and made adjustments to their asset allocations, but every single one of them includes all five asset classes in their plans. Modern portfolio theory and real world experience tell us that an optimal portfolio cannot be built without the extraordinarily strong foundation of cash, fixed-income, equities, real estate and absolute return investments.

For the remainder of the book, we're going to talk about how the five asset classes can be fitted together to construct your optimal retirement plan. When your plan is built upon a solid foundation, it will stand the test of time and provide comfort and security for your family indefinitely. It's time to see what your pension plan will look like.

Summary

- The two pillars of modern portfolio theory are diversification and understanding risk. The great pension plans use this foundation to build their investment portfolios.
- Stanford University's William Sharpe, based much of his work on modern portfolio theory. In 1990, he was named a co-winner of the Nobel Prize in Economics. His research proved that in a properly diversified investment portfolio, individual investment selection, market timing and luck were virtually irrelevant factors in the overall return. Sharpe found that over ninety percent of an investor's lifetime return can be attributed to asset allocation.
- If the individual investments you pick perform somewhere near average, if you don't try to time the market, if you simply have average luck and if you add to that a competent job of asset allocation, your investment portfolio will reward you by earning something like ninety-seven percent of the maximum it could be expected to earn. Where I come from, ninety-seven percent is a good grade.
- Historically, investors have underperformed the markets, due to poor asset allocation. During the greatest bull market of all time, from 1984 to 2000, the average stock fund had a return of 14.0 percent per year, while the average investor earned only 5.3 percent.
- A properly diversified portfolio that includes all five asset classes, will have a higher rate of return and a lower level of risk over the long term than any one of the asset classes could provide on its own.
- Over the long term, cash is generally the worst-performing asset class, however, it's an indispensable part of diversification. During rare periods when stocks and bonds fall in tandem, cash is invariably the strongest performing asset class.
- The fixed-income asset class is made up of CDs, bonds and preferred shares. With all three of these investment types the return is fixed, hence the title "fixed-income" for the asset class.
- If your portfolio consists of 100 percent fixed-income, your chances of long-term success are slim to none and slim just left

town. The historical real return for bonds has been about 3.5 percent, before tax. After tax, the real return hovers around one percent.

• Fixed-income investments are, by themselves, poison to the long-term investor. They'll safely store the purchasing power of your money, but that's about it. Fixed-income simply can't be counted on to deliver the type of real return that will provide your family with safety and comfort over the long term. If you're healthy and under sixty-five years of age or married and under seventy-five years of age, then you're a long-term investor, like it or not.

• Many investors labour under the misconception that high interest rates are good for fixed-income investors. I call this the illusion of safety and it's perhaps one of the most dangerous fallacies the investing public is faced with today. Our tax system punishes fixed-income investors. The higher the interest rate, the worse the real return after tax.

• In the capitalist system, owners will always beat loaners. There are two reasons why this is true. First, businesses wouldn't borrow money unless they thought they were going to make a profit. Second, if owners don't make more money than lenders over the long term, they can't pay lenders back.

• Fixed-income has an important role to play in the construction of your optimum portfolio, but you must understand that too much of a good thing can be deadly.

• The fixed-income asset class is made up of five subclasses. These subclasses are: government bonds, CDs, corporate bonds, preferred shares and foreign bonds. Each subclass has advantages and disadvantages, additionally they each help to reduce or eliminate at least one of the five big risks.

• If the hundreds of investment systems and strategies you see on the news, in magazines and in books work so well, then why aren't any pension funds using them?

• When it comes to building the equity portion of a pension plan, there are only five points you need to understand:

1. Over the very long term, stocks will always be the highest performing asset class.
2. Over the very long term, stocks are the "safest" asset class.
3. Short-term volatility is not real risk.
4. You cannot outsmart the equity markets.
5. Rebalancing is the key.

• Over the long term, volatility disappears, and risk becomes the chance you'll fail to achieve your goals.

• Out of the five big risks, the most dangerous is inflation. Equities are the only asset class completely immune to inflation. In the short term, they may be volatile, but in the long term, they help eliminate inflation risk. Many people consider equities risky, but because they can help eliminate the largest obstacle inflation standing between your family and its goals, they are in fact, in real terms, the safest of the asset classes.

• If the short-term or even the medium-term prices of equities were predictable, then the returns would be the same as fixed-income. The more unpredictable the short-term prices of equities, the higher the long-term returns will be. Volatility is our friend.

• Investors confuse volatility and risk because of panic. The real risk for these people is their own behaviour.

• The great pension plans profit from short-term volatility through rebalancing. When pensions rebalance, they take a portion of the profits from the stronger-performing asset classes and use it to buy more of the temporarily underperforming asset class. In other words, they sell high and buy low.

• In order to make effective use of equities, there are only three concepts you need to grasp:

1. why you need them
2. what they will do for you
3. why they will always work

• There's only one predictor of stock price that consistently and accurately works over time: the value of the company. The real value of a company is its earnings power.

• Over time, the earnings of a good quality company are going to grow in four ways:

1. inflation
2. the growth of the Gross Domestic Product (GDP)
3. retained earnings
4. growth of the business

• If you feel, as I do, that a secure retirement includes the option of remaining in your home for as long as you choose, then the value of your house should not be included in your asset allocation.

• Real estate helps to lower the overall risk level of your portfolio because it helps to reduce and eliminate inflation risk, interest rate risk, market risk and manager risk. Real estate is also one of the easiest asset classes for investors to hold through tough times.

• The great pension plans don't manage real estate investments directly. Instead, they utilize professional property managers. Real Estate Investment Trusts (REITs) also make use of professional property managers. For most North American investors, these vehicles represent the best method of investing directly in real estate.

• REITs most commonly invest in office buildings, shopping malls, apartment buildings, hotels and retirement homes. Most pensions prefer apartment buildings, office buildings and shopping malls, because of their relatively stable income streams.

• When investing in real estate, most pensions look for a return on their capital that's roughly 4.50 percent higher than the current thirty-year government bond rate.

• Absolute return investments are designed to reach a target annual return, regardless of movement in the stock or bond markets. As a general rule, they're immune to movements in interest rates and inflation. The two main categories of absolute return investments are real return bonds and absolute return funds.

• Real return bonds have both their principal and interest payments indexed to the Consumer Price Index (CPI).

• Absolute return funds are commonly referred to as market neutral hedge funds. They're described as market neutral because their strategies act to remove the broad movements of the equity and bond markets from their returns. The managers of these funds work to capture and profit from price inefficiencies in the financial markets.

- High minimum investment requirements usually keep individual investors from including absolute returns in their asset allocation. The advent of the "fund of funds" concept provides the solution to this problem.
- There's always a temptation among individual investors to omit one or more asset classes from their portfolios. Avoid this mistake.

Chapter Seven

What Does the Ideal Pension Plan Look Like?

Common sense is the collection of prejudices acquired by age eighteen.
—Albert Einstein

We've covered the five big risks as well as the five major asset classes. Those were admittedly some of the drier topics in pension management, but they're necessary topics if you're going to understand the big picture. I don't expect you to be an expert by this point, but I do hope you understand and accept that the five asset classes, when combined, can produce for you a lower total level of risk than any one of the asset classes could provide on its own. This is powerful stuff! It excites me and I hope it's starting to excite you.

So what does the optimal pension plan look like? As you know by now, the optimal plan incorporates all five major asset classes.

1. cash
2. fixed-income
3. equities
4. investment real estate
5. absolute return investments

In graphic form, it would look something like the following:

THE FIVE MAJOR ASSET CLASSES (FIG. 11)

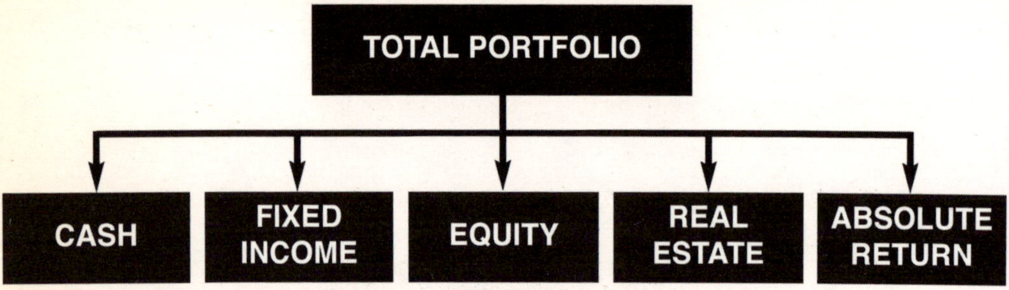

Back in Chapter 5, we learned that diversification is one of the keys to the success of modern portfolio theory. By diversifying your overall portfolio into the five major asset classes, you're implementing the first level of diversification. Dividing your portfolio into five asset classes isn't enough to completely eliminate market risk, but it will act to severely dampen the short-term oscillations of the various markets.

In order to continue their quest to reduce risk, pension plans have found it necessary to incorporate additional layers of diversification. Returning to Chapter 4, the five big risks are:

1. currency risk
2. interest rate risk
3. inflation risk
4. specific or manager risk
5. systematic or market risk

The great pension plans act to further reduce risk and volatility in their portfolios, by diversifying four of the five major asset classes yet again. (There's little to be gained by diversifying a cash position.)

Fixed income is diversified into four subclasses: government bonds, municipal bonds, corporate bonds and preferred shares or preferred securities.

Remember that we covered each of these in the Asset Allocation and Fixed-Income section of Chapter 5. If you need to refresh your memory, feel free to take a break for some quick review.

The fixed-income asset class thus looks something like this:

THE FOUR SUB-CLASSES OF FIXED INCOME (FIG. 12)

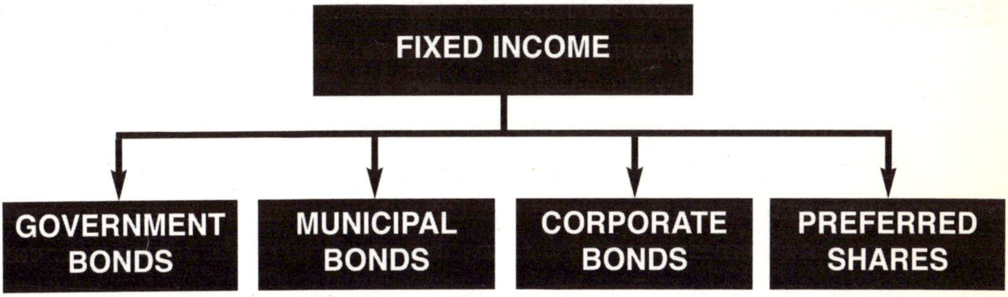

Both the equity and investment real estate asset classes are given not one, but two additional levels of diversification by the great pension funds. In order to be as certain as possible that manager, market and currency risks have been eliminated from the equity asset class, the managers of the great pension plans diversity first by the subclass of geography, into US equity, European equity and global equity.

The first subclass of equity could be shown graphically as:

THE THREE SUB-CLASSES OF EQUITY (FIG. 13)

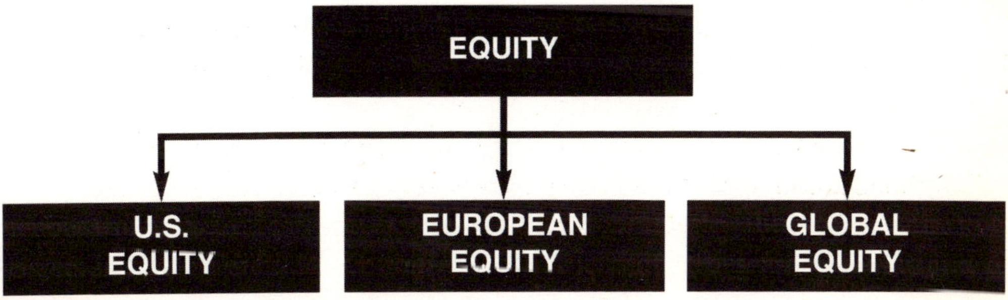

Once the equity asset class has been diversified geographically, pensions proceed to add yet another level of diversification by breaking each geographic region—America, European and global—into their own subclasses. These two subclasses are value and growth.

Value companies are typically companies that are currently out of favor for one reason or another. Perhaps their industry isn't doing well as a whole or perhaps the company's going through tough times. A good value manager can identify when the market price of a stock has dropped significantly below the real value of the company. When this happens, he'll invest with the intention of taking a profit as the company's situation inevitably improves. Value managers often refer to what they do as buying a dollar in assets for fifty cents.

Growth managers tend to take the opposite tack. They don't care so much about what they pay for a company, as how fast it will grow. The prevailing thought among growth managers is that if a company is growing quickly, the market price of its stock will eventually follow.

Typically, value and growth advocates each think the other is nuts. Value managers can't understand why anyone would buy a stock, unless they were paying less than the real value of the company. Growth managers, on the other hand, think that value fans are living in the past.

Who's right? You may be surprised to hear that they both are. Over the long term, the returns provided by the growth and value strategies are nearly identical. What does differ sharply, however, are the periods in which each tends to provide its returns. Take a look at the next chart. It shows the average returns of the growth and value strategies, relative to each other, over the past twenty-five years.

VALUE VS. GROWTH STOCKS (FIG. 14)

Annual Relative Performance of Value vs. Growth 1975-2003

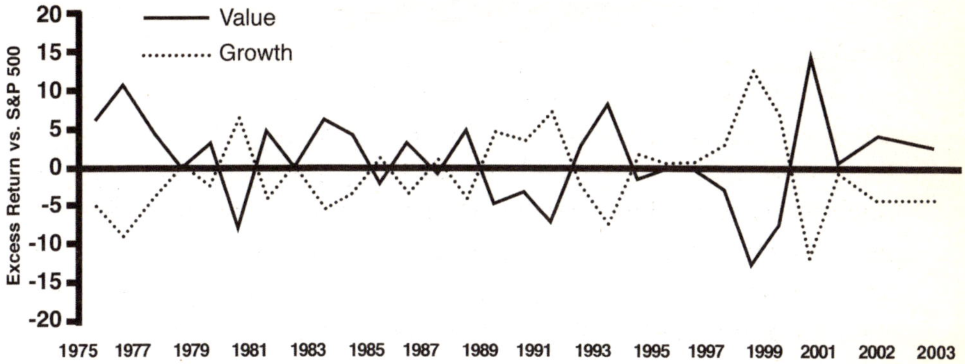

Growth: S&P Barra Growth Index
Value: S&P Barra Value Index

Surprising isn't it? Each strategy had a fairly volatile ride on its own, yet they ended up posting almost identical returns. By combining the growth and value strategies equally within a pension plan, the great managers are able to slash the level of volatility without compromising the returns one little bit. Taking a layered approach to diversification has helped pension funds reduce and eliminate risk for decades. It will work for you too, if you let it.

With the extra layer of diversification, the equity asset class ends up looking something like this:

THE COMPLETE EQUITY ASSET CLASS (FIG. 15)

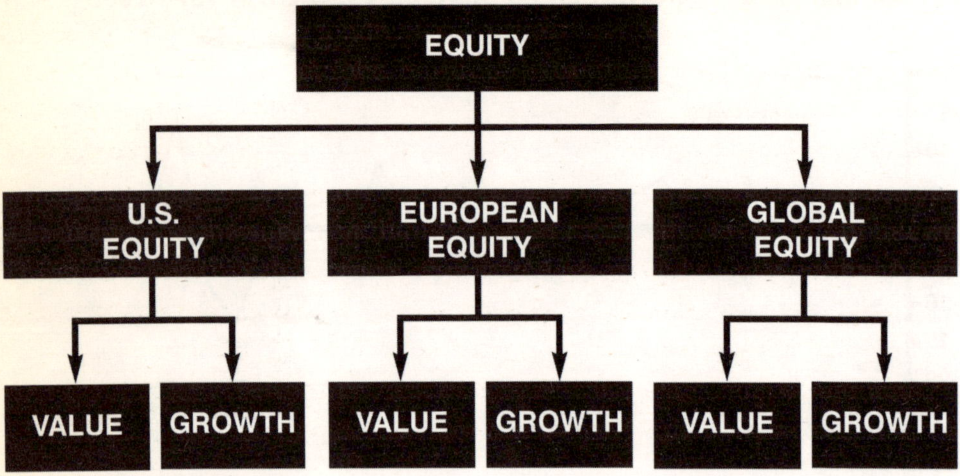

The investment real estate asset class is treated in a similar fashion to the equity class. It's diversified through two separate layers. Each level of diversification further reduces risk and volatility. The first layer of additional diversification is by geography. The second layer of diversification is by type. The main types of investment real estate we want to consider are: retail (shopping malls), office buildings and residential (apartment buildings).

I'm sure you've experienced, on a personal level, the fluctuations that can take place in the real estate marketplace. Most of us have either seen the value of our own home drop temporarily over some period of time or we've heard the story first-hand from a friend who's had the experience. Because of the relatively long period of time it takes for a real estate transaction to take place, real estate tends to have much less volatility than the equity markets. Less volatility is not to say there is no volatility however, hence our rationale for additional layers of diversification.

The great pension fund managers know something that you don't know and it may surprise you. Yes, real estate can experience volatility and it can occasionally fall in value, but since the end of World War II, when the government first began keeping track of real estate prices, there has never been a single year when a properly diversified portfolio of North American real estate declined in value. Not one year. Individual regions decline in value; in fact it happens almost every year. Likewise, individual types of real estate have dropped in value, but not one single year has the average price of North American real estate as a whole, dropped in value. Given enough time, all things are possible, so I'm sure it will happen someday, but am I worried about it? Are the great pension plans worried about it? Heck no! As we diversify your plan through the use of the five asset classes, we eliminate risks; as we add each additional layer of diversification to each individual asset class, we continue to reduce volatility and eliminate risks. Modern portfolio theory makes it happen for the great pension plans and modern portfolio theory can make it happen for your personal plan as well.

The real estate investment class ends up looking something like this:

THE COMPLETE REAL ESTATE ASSET CLASS (FIG. 16)

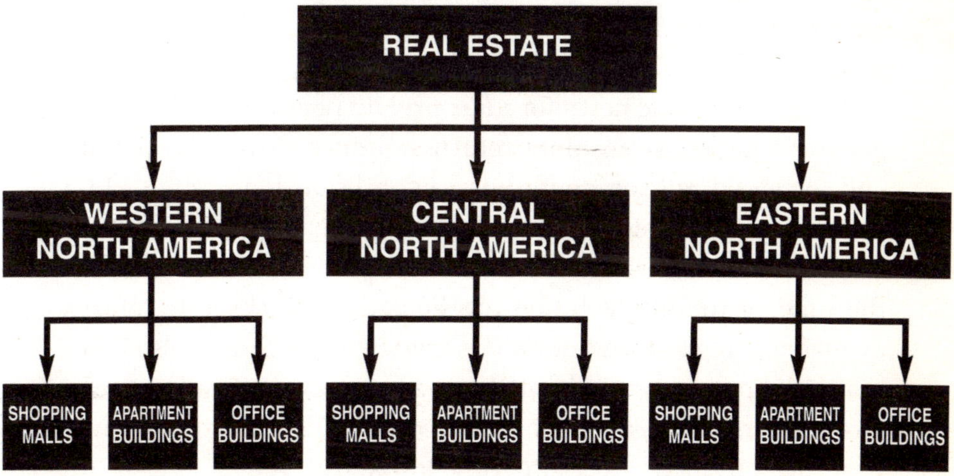

Unlike the equity and real estate asset classes, the absolute return asset class doesn't require a layer of geographic diversification. Why? Well, as you may recall, the absolute return asset class isn't nearly as prone to currency risk, interest rate risk, inflation risk or market risk as the other four asset classes are. In fact, of the five big risks, manager risk is the only one that poses a serious threat to absolute returns.

In Chapter 4, we learned that the term "manager risk" describes the possibility that the investment manager will perform worse than the average manager in his field. Since any pension fund would perform significant research into the background, philosophy and performance history of a manager before making a decision to invest, there's little real danger that the manager is bad at his or her job. Rather, manager risk arises from the chance that an error in judgment could occur or that a decision may have unforeseen negative consequences.

The absolute return asset class is one of my personal favorites. I get the same warm and fuzzy feeling from it as some people may get from a cherished old sweater. In my opinion, no other asset class makes as much of a contribution to reducing and eliminating risk as this one. The trade-off for all the positive benefits that absolute returns bring to your plan is manager risk. Fortunately for us, manager risk, as we learned earlier, can be controlled through diversification.

This is fantastic news for your private pension plan. You can get the benefits of absolute returns—reduced overall volatility and increased returns—with no drawbacks, as long as we add a second layer of diversification to the absolute return asset class to bring manager risk under control. In Chapter 6, we discussed how the fund of funds revolution has helped make absolute returns available to regular investors. The fund of funds format also automatically provides much of the manager diversification we're looking for. Asset allocation and diversification are very simple concepts, but their effects are truly wonderful.

The absolute return asset class will end up looking something like this, after the second layer of diversification is added:

THE ABSOLUTE RETURN ASSET CLASSES (FIG. 17)

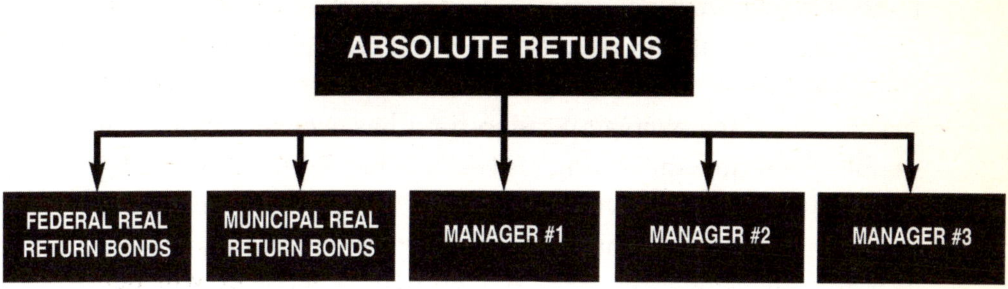

For decades, pension plans have known that the absolute return asset class can help reduce the volatility and the risk of their portfolios, while adding to long-term returns. The great managers consider this asset class one of the most important weapons in their arsenal. Now you have it too, but it won't do you any good unless you use it.

* * *

I hope that by now, you're starting to get your head around the concept that each asset class in its own way contributes to reducing your risk, reducing short-term volatility and increasing your long-term returns. This is perhaps the single most important concept to grasp in the journey to effective pension management. As you add each of the five asset classes to your portfolio, risk will continue to decrease and long-term returns will improve. Forgive me if I'm being repetitive here, but this is important. Again, every asset class helps to reduce risk and increase long-term returns.

There is no scenario where it's better to leave out an asset class. If you're saying to yourself, "I do need a pension and I hear what you're saying, but I can't take the risk of adding equities to my pension, so I'll just stick to the other four asset classes," then you're missing the point. The great pension plans and Nobel Prize-winning modern portfolio theory both tell us that there's less risk in including all five asset classes in your portfolio than there is in including only one. Or two, or three, or even four. And it's not just a little less risk. According to data provided by RBC BENCHMARK® and Dalbar, Inc. and Lipper Inc. over the past twenty years, the average pension fund has achieved more than double the return the average investor achieved, while exposing themselves to only a fraction of the risk. In Chapter 4, we defined risk as the chance that you'll fail to achieve your investment goals. The great pension plans may not provide an exciting ride, but they achieve their goals. More than half of individual investors, have put their futures in the hands of a haphazardly designed portfolio, completely lacking a plan, based more on their fears or their greed than any rational thought process, which has no real mathematical chance of achieving success. How's that for risk?

As we add each asset class to your plan, we continue to reduce your risk and improve your returns. As we diversify each asset class into subclasses, we further reduce and eliminate risks and volatility, while improving your returns yet again. The great pension plans achieve their goals and you will too—if you can use the five major asset classes to your advantage.

I promised you that in this chapter we'd see what the properly designed pension fund looks like. So far, we've addressed each of the individual parts of the plan. We've seen what it looks like when each of the five major asset classes is properly diversified into subclasses. It's time to take a look at the full picture. The completed pension plan, shown in Figure 18 and assembled from the components that we've just studied, contains a total of twenty-seven different asset classes and subclasses. There's nothing new here; I've just taken all the pieces we talked about and placed them together on one chart. Take some time with this. Get a good feel for it. Remember that each asset class and each additional subclass helps to reduce and eliminate risk. A total of twenty-seven times we've reduced risk and improved returns. The combined effect is powerful, to say the least.

COMPLETE PENSION ASSET ALLOCATION (FIG. 18)

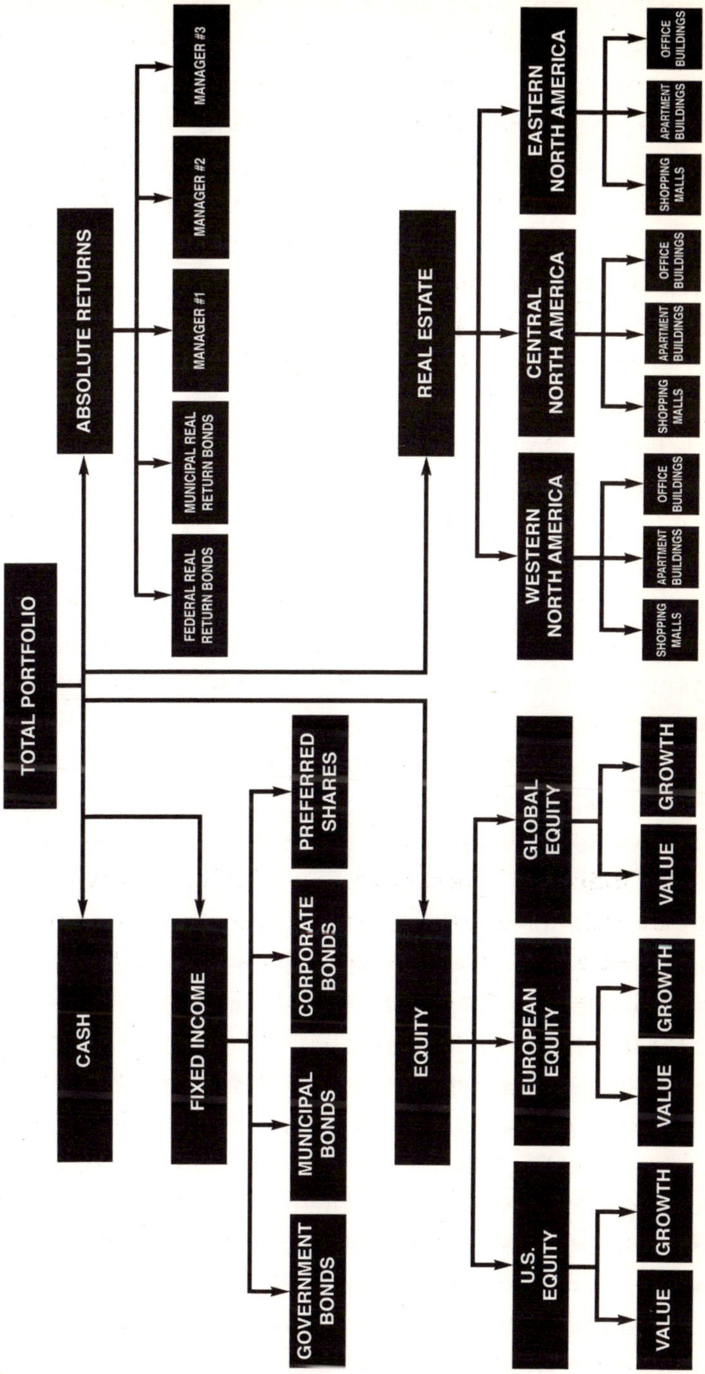

Thus far in this book, I've talked only in generalities about asset allocation. I've shown you which asset classes to use, why you want to use them and how they work. But what I haven't shown you is the proper way to divide your portfolio between them. I had good reason for this. I promised you at the beginning of this book that I'd keep things as simple as I possibly could, and to do that, I've refrained from addressing the issue of actually dividing your portfolio into the five major asset classes. That changes now. I don't want to give you the impression that I held off because this is a complicated topic, because it's not. On the contrary, it really couldn't be more black and white.

For retirement investing, there's really only one best asset allocation: the optimal portfolio.

I know you've been told repeatedly over the years that everyone's needs are unique. It's true; everyone's needs are unique, just as everyone's specific goals are unique. But I fear that, just as with many other facets of investing, the relative importance of this point has been blown out of proportion. Meeting your unique needs does not necessarily require a completely unique solution.

There are literally millions of possible combinations of investments available and there are millions of people who belong to pension plans. So why then are these plans all so similar when it comes to asset allocation and investment strategy? They have millions of members and each of those members has "unique" needs and goals. Why do all these pensions succeed in meeting these millions of unique goals using asset allocations that are so similar? Modern portfolio theory.

Modern portfolio theory tells us that as we add asset classes and layers of diversification, we're reducing and eliminating risk, while improving long-term returns. Markowitz said: for every given level of risk, there exists a portfolio that will produce the maximum possible expected return, and conversely, for any given targeted return, there exists a portfolio which holds the lowest possible risk.

Remember the efficient frontier? The efficient frontier graphically shows which portfolios offer the best possible value.

EFFICIENT FRONTIER (FIG. 19)

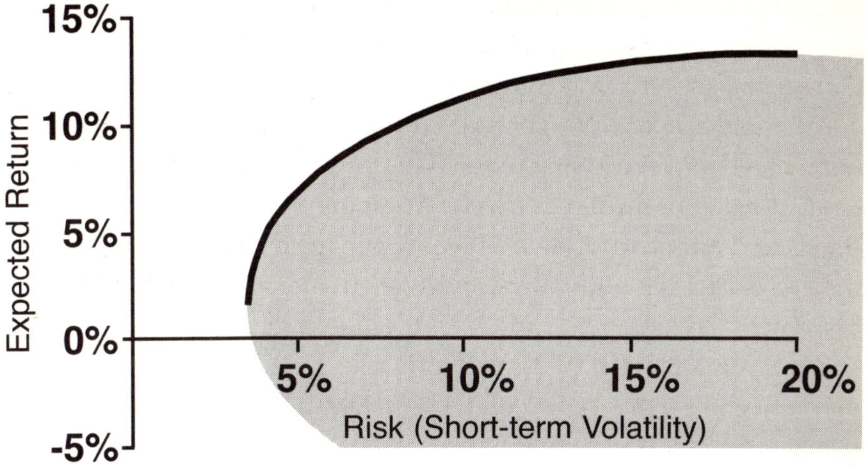

SOURCE: CIBC Wood Gundy Private Client Investing

Investment portfolios that lie directly on the efficient frontier are perfect portfolios, in that they require the lowest possible amount of risk for a given targeted return and they provide the maximum possible expected return for a given level of risk. But there are still hundreds of portfolios that lie on the efficient frontier. Do we want to target a return of 8.0 percent or 8.1 percent? Many advisors recommend that you calculate the return that is required to meet all your goals, then simply choose the spot on the efficient frontier that provides that return. I have no quarrel with this strategy; it will, after all, almost certainly help you achieve your goals.

On the other hand, I'm an even bigger fan of efficiency, as are the great pension plans. The portfolio I want to own is the one that offers the absolute best combination of risk and return. We'll talk more about this soon, but first take a look back at the graph of the efficient frontier. Looking at that, where do you think the best combination of risk to return lies?

Most people innately do a good job of picking out a point on the efficient frontier that offers a very good combination of risk and return. I wouldn't be at all surprised if you looked at the graph and dropped your finger right on the optimum location. Our brains are amazing things.

If we didn't want to choose our location on the efficient frontier by feel, however, what would we do? I can assure you that the great pension plans never choose anything by feel. They like formulas and equations that tell them to the third decimal place that they're doing the right thing with their members' hard-earned retirement savings.

Not surprisingly, pension funds use a mathematical tool to pinpoint the exact location on the efficient frontier that offers the single most efficient combination of risk (volatility) to return. You may be expecting a complex equation at this point, but I have a pleasant surprise for you. All you need to find the portfolio with the single best combination of risk and return is a straight line. This line was originally postulated in 1958 by James Tobin and is called the capital market line. On the graph of the efficient frontier, the capital market line is simply a line that starts at the "risk-free rate" (defined by Tobin as the current interest rate of ninety-day government bonds) and runs tangent to the efficient frontier. If you've been out of math class for a while, the tangent is the point on a graph where a straight line would only touch one point on the graph.

James Tobin called the ninety-day government bond rate the risk-free rate, because ninety-day government bonds are widely considered as the safest way to protect the purchasing power of money over short periods of time. The point at which a straight line drawn from the risk-free rate would just touch the graph of the efficient frontier represents the single best mathematical combination of risk and return. As I mentioned previously, pension funds like numbers. James Tobin's capital market line allows funds to calculate with mathematical certainty which asset allocation, from the almost infinite number available, can offer their members the best value.

CAPITAL MARKET LINE (FIG. 20)

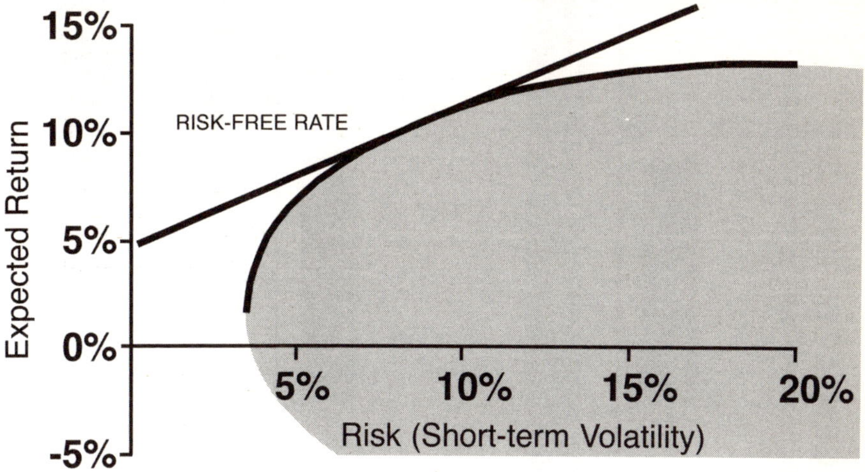

SOURCE: CIBC Wood Gundy Private Client Investing

The point where the capital market line just touches the efficient frontier is the point of maximum efficiency. The investment portfolio corresponding to this point is the most efficient possible portfolio. James Tobin named this portfolio "the super efficient portfolio" because it offers the best possible combination of risk and return. To answer my earlier question, this is why pension funds look alike. The funds want to do the best job that they can for their members. They perform their own due diligence, they hold their own strategy meetings and they make their own independent decisions, but in the end, those decisions look eerily similar. They look similar because invariably, they want to run their plan efficiently. They want the lowest level of volatility (short-term risk) and the best return they can achieve. I want nothing less than the same for you.

Using Markowitz's modern portfolio theory and James Tobin's capital market line, we can find, what I believe to be, the optimal asset allocation. It's shown below.

PENSION ASSET ALLOCATION WITH PERCENTAGES (FIG. 21)

The percentage of the portfolio allocated to each asset class is divided equally among the sub-class below it.

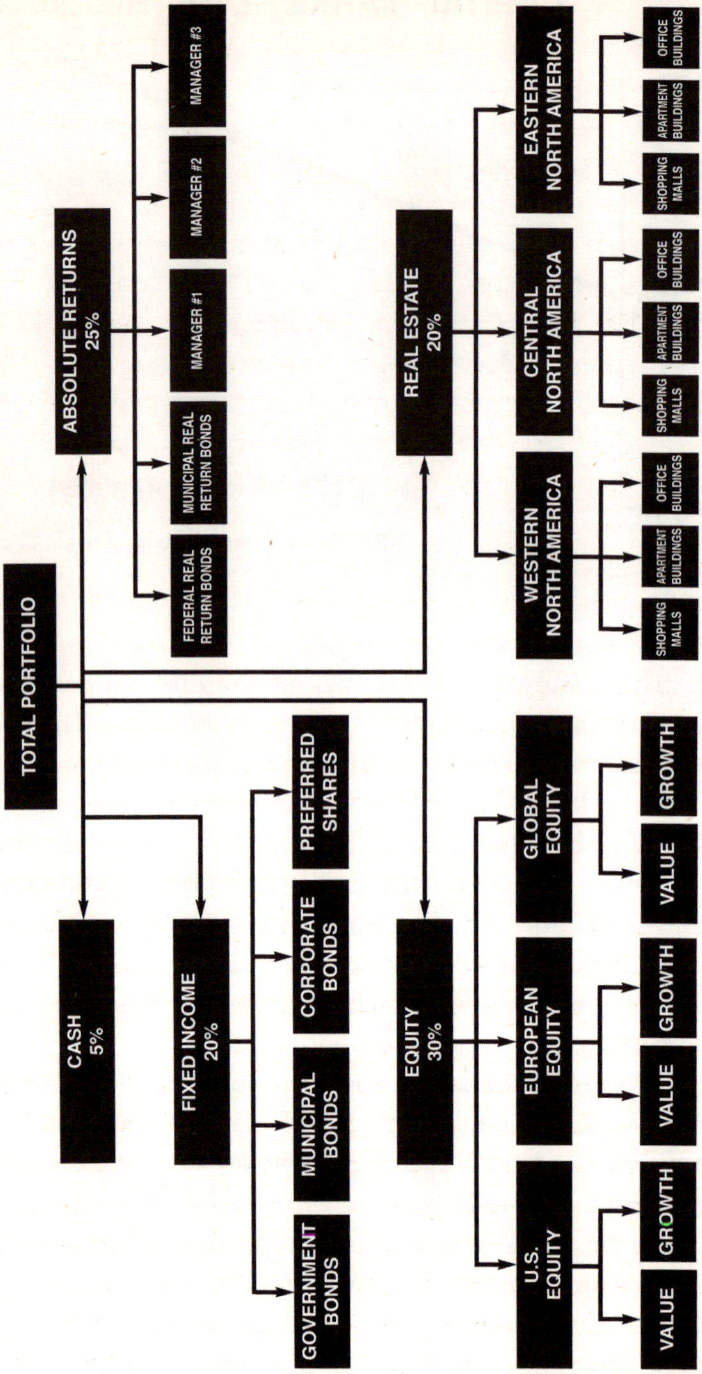

The work of Markowitz, Sharpe and Tobin, tells us that if you want efficiency, your retirement plan should contain five percent cash, twenty percent fixed-income, thirty percent equities, twenty percent investment real estate and twenty-five percent absolute return investments.

Is this the portfolio everyone should have? No. You have to be completely comfortable with your portfolio. Make no mistake, relative to what most investors do with their money, there's not much risk in this portfolio, but there's still some risk. There are risks present in everything and although some can be eliminated and all can be reduced, it simply isn't possible to dispense with risk altogether. However, as a general rule, if your head is in the right place and you'd be comfortable having your investments 100 percent in bonds, then you should be comfortable with the optimal portfolio—the volatility is similar.

As I just said, the volatility of the optimally designed plan is about the same as that of bonds. The risk, however, is quite another thing. As you recall, we're defining risk as the chance that you'll fail to achieve your goals. In the short term, the optimal pension portfolio and bonds have about the same amount of volatility; in the long term, however, the optimal portfolio will tend to produce an after-inflation return, or real return, of about five times what bonds have historically produced. Five times the returns with similar volatility. Where's the risk in that? Is there a better chance that you'll fail to meet your goals (risk, as we define it) if you're receiving the real return of bonds or if you're receiving five times that amount?

That being said, not everyone can or should own the optimal portfolio. Many of you should, and all of you would probably make more money if you did, but nonetheless it's a personal decision. Perhaps you have some big one-time expenses in the near future, maybe your health is poor and you feel there really isn't a long term in the cards for you or maybe you're just so emotionally scarred from terrible advice and decisions in your past that you don't think you could deal with even the minimal short-term volatility of the optimal portfolio.

The reasons don't matter. What matters is your comfort. At the start of this journey, I told you that using a pension strategy could provide comfort and safety for your family. It will, but everyone's idea of comfort is different. We are, after all, unique. If you search your soul and decide that you need, for your own peace of mind, less volatility, that's fine. Yes, you'll potentially give up some returns, but comfort and peace of mind are equally important.

Adjusting Asset Allocation to Your Risk Tolerance (Comfort Level)

If, for example, your unique situation requires twenty percent less volatility than bonds (because remember that the optimal portfolio delivers about that amount of volatility), do you scrap the optimal portfolio? No. If you want twenty percent less short-term volatility, the solution is as simple as cash. Simply reduce the size of your fixed-income, equity, real estate and absolute return asset classes by twenty percent each. The balance is used to increase the size of your cash position. Two minutes of work on a calculator will give you the asset allocation that's optimal for you. Fifteen percent less short-term volatility? Thirty? The process is identical. If you change your asset allocation proportionately in this way, your expected long-term return will, of course, drop, but at least you can have the confidence that comes with knowing that you're still going to receive the maximum possible return for the given level of short-term volatility you've selected.

You never need to use any other asset classes and you never need to use any other strategies. If your comfort dictates that short-term volatility be reduced, then increase the cash. Your short-term volatility will be lower and you can still expect the maximum possible return for that level of volatility. It really isn't rocket science; it's just modern portfolio theory.

At this point, you should understand what a pension plan actually looks like and why they're so gosh darn effective. Once again, I think you should take a moment to congratulate yourself.

There's been a lot of information and a few tough concepts, but if you're still reading, then you're still hanging in there. Good work.

Before I conclude this chapter, I feel I need to clarify one point. My goal in writing this book is to allow you to retire in comfort and safety. As I define it, the optimal pension portfolio is very safe. Over the long term (and you have to be pretty long-in-the-tooth not to have a long term), the higher relative returns that the optimal pension portfolio can provide, will give you a considerably higher margin for error than you'd have with less efficient, and therefore lower returning, portfolios. Long-term risk is the chance that we'll fail to meet our goals. Targeting higher returns reduces this risk, while lower returns increase it. When we choose to target lower, long-term returns in order to experience less short-term volatility now, we're inadvertently increasing our long-term risk.

I want you to do something for me. I want you to look forward. Imagine that you're eighty years old. Both you and your spouse have been blessed—you're both healthy, you've raised a wonderful family and your lives have been happy and fulfilling. You do have one problem, however. You're running out of money. For the first time in decades, finances have once again become the main subject of conversation around the dinner table. Sacrifices and lifestyle changes have to be made, trips postponed, perhaps permanently. I want you to really imagine your family in this situation. Do you think there's any chance that you'll be saying to yourself, "I'm glad I chose less short-term volatility thirty years ago?" Or will you be thinking, "Instead of taking the risk of running out of money now, when I can least afford it, I should've learned to accept just a bit more temporary short-term volatility when I was younger."

Just food for thought. Take from it what you will.

The balance between comfort and safety is indeed a difficult balance to achieve. Choose 100 percent safety now and I can virtually guarantee your long-term failure. Choose a portfolio made up of 100 percent stocks and I can guarantee you a lot of sleepless nights. Before you decide to deviate from the optimal pension portfolio, consider that it is, after all, optimal. Risk and volatility can be scary words, but when it comes to the optimal pension portfolio, try to keep it in perspective. The optimal portfolio carries about the same amount of short-term risk (volatility) as bonds. The safe haven of choice for many nervous and scared investors is CDs, but as we saw in Chapter 6, CDs are, in their essence, bonds.

As we've learned, the most efficient way to balance the short-term risk of volatility with long-term safety lies with the optimal portfolio. If you're so sure that you need to avoid short-term volatility that you're willing to sacrifice long-term safety, then by all means go ahead. Your comfort is important, but please consider the possibility that your perception could be colored by bad experiences from the past. I respectfully submit that you owe it to yourself and to the long-term security of your family, to carefully consider why you feel this way. Sometimes it's necessary to cast a light on dark places.

Summary

• Pension funds desire the lowest possible risk and the highest possible return, in other words, they strive for efficiency. In order to accomplish this goal, they reduce and eliminate each risk as much as possible. Each of the five major asset classes is further diversified, through the addition of at least two subclasses. Each additional layer of diversification continues to reduce risk and incrementally increase returns.

• The completed pension plan contains a total of twenty-seven different asset classes and subclasses.

• James Tobin postulated that for pension investing, there's really only one best asset allocation. He named this portfolio "the super efficient portfolio." The super efficient portfolio is found by drawing a straight line on the graph of the efficient frontier, extending from the current risk-free rate (ninety-day government T-bill rate) tangent to the efficient frontier. The point at which the straight line touches a single point on the curve marks the location of the super efficient portfolio. In a nutshell, this is the reason why all pension funds use similar strategies.

• The super efficient portfolio is subject to about the same level of short-term volatility as a laddered bond portfolio. If you're comfortable with owning bonds, you should be comfortable with this optimal portfolio.

• Over the long term, the real return of the optimal portfolio should be roughly five times the real return provided by a bond portfolio. Is there a better chance that you'll fail to meet your goals (risk, as we define it), if you're receiving the real return of bonds or if you're targeting five times that amount?

• If your own personal circumstances dictate that less short-term risk is necessary, then James Tobin's capital market line offers a simple and elegant solution—cash. By reducing the size of the fixed-income, equity, real estate and absolute return asset classes that make up the optimal portfolio in equal proportion, and increasing your cash level correspondingly, your risk level will be reduced by that same proportion. Your return will still be the maximum possible return for the given level of short-term volatility you've selected. No other asset classes or strategies are ever necessary.

• The balance between comfort and safety is a difficult balance to achieve. Choose 100 percent safety now and your long-term failure is all but assured. Choose a portfolio made up of 100 percent stocks and you'll have sleepless nights. The most efficient path to achieve balance between short-term volatility and long-term safety lies with the optimal portfolio.

CHAPTER EIGHT

Portfolio Rebalancing: The Art of Dynamic Asset Allocation

To every thing there is a season, and a time to every purpose under heaven.
—Ecclesiastes 3:1

The point of asset allocation and diversification is reducing risk and increasing returns. Both of these tactics work beautifully, and as you've seen, both are key parts of modern portfolio theory. By utilizing all the tools we've learned so far in this book, the overall risk level of your portfolio can be reduced by leaps and bounds. The great pension plans generate average returns like the stock market, with short-term volatility levels comparable to bonds. But it gets even better.

Pension funds know another trick for increasing returns still further, while cutting short-term volatility even more. You really have to hand it to them, don't you?

Using a technique often referred to as dynamic asset allocation, pension managers shave an additional ten to twenty percent off the already minimal risk level of the optimal portfolio. On average, dynamic asset allocation also improves the long-term return of the portfolio by about 2.5 percent. It's a beautiful thing!

How does dynamic asset allocation work? When you get right down to it, dynamic asset allocation is really just a fancy term for rebalancing. As you know, the five major asset classes in the optimal portfolio aren't highly correlated; they don't go up and down at exactly the same time. During any given year, one or more of the asset classes may experience a temporary decline in market value, while the rest may rise in market value. As the asset classes change in value relative to each other, the portfolio becomes less optimal. Remember that for any given level of risk, there's only *one* portfolio that offers the highest possible expected level of return. Therefore, as the values of the individual asset classes change due to the effects of short-term volatility, the portfolio will slowly become less and less efficient. In the industry, we refer to this effect as "portfolio drift." Rebalancing is the most effective cure.

There are two primary reasons why even an optimally designed portfolio will drift. The first reason is short-term volatility. We've discussed this effect previously in the book and by now I'm sure you realize that far from being something to be concerned about, short-term volatility actually works in our favor. The second cause of portfolio drift is equally unavoidable: each asset class has a different long-term rate of return. We learned in Chapter 6 that historically, no other asset class can match the return of equities over the long term. If the portfolio isn't rebalanced periodically, the proportion allocated to equities will keep growing and growing as they continually outpace the returns of the other four asset classes. Many investors are content to allow their equities to grow unchecked. They rationalize that since they've already made a significant profit, they can afford to take more risk. I have a problem with this attitude and if you've been paying attention, so should you. Which asset class has the highest level of short-term volatility? The answer is, of course, equities. If the proportion of the portfolio allocated to any one asset class changes, so too does the amount of short-term volatility. Pension funds and conservative investors want to avoid risk wherever possible, so pension funds and conservative investors rebalance.

Recall that the optimal portfolio is made up of five percent cash, twenty percent fixed-income, thirty percent equities, twenty percent investment real estate and twenty-five percent absolute return investments. Inevitably, as time progresses, these percentages will change. Even if all five asset classes have a great year, some will still do better than others and that will change the asset mix of the portfolio. Six months after your pension portfolio is implemented, it might look something like this: three percent cash, eighteen percent fixed-income, thirty-four percent equities, eighteen percent investment real estate and twenty-seven percent absolute return investments.

Regardless of the performance of your portfolio, the market values of the five asset classes will change relative to each other. None of your asset classes necessarily needs to drop in value for this to occur; it may be that every asset class gains in value, but if some asset classes rise in value more than others, then the percentage of your portfolio allocated to each asset class will change. The opposite is true as well: even if every asset class drops in value, some will drop more or less than others and the allocation of your portfolio will change. Both of these extreme results are fairly uncommon, however. Most of the time, you'll find yourself somewhere in the middle.

Great investment managers look at this and see an opportunity. How often have you heard the old adage: "buy low and sell high"? It's not easy to do, is it? Professional investment managers use fluctuations in the portfolio's asset mix as an opportunity to sell high and buy low. It means the same thing, but it's the other way around. Look at the last sample portfolio again. The equities have gained four percent relative to the other asset classes. The fixed income has dropped two percent relative to the other asset classes. By rebalancing the portfolio back to the optimal asset allocation where it started, what are we doing? We're effectively selling four percent of the equities at a profit (selling high), selling two percent of the absolute return investments (selling high again) and restoring the cash, fixed-income and real estate back to their original percentages (buying low).

It's virtually impossibly to "buy low and sell high" over the short term. The random fluctuations of the markets make the risk too great to justify the potential return. It is, however, not only possible, but dead simple, to "sell high and buy low." All we have to do is rebalance back to the optimal asset allocation that we started with, and as if by magic, we've taken profits on our best performing investments and bought more of our lagging asset classes at discount prices. Welcome to the world of dynamic asset allocation.

Rebalancing is a vital component of our asset allocation policy. What would be the point of knowing what the optimal pension portfolio looks like, if we didn't periodically ensure that our portfolio still reflects it?

Twice per year, you need to have a conversation with your financial advisor and compare your portfolio with your optimal asset allocation target. When you're comparing them, it's a simple matter to see what changes need to be made in order to return to the optimal portfolio. When it comes to rebalancing, I can assure you that if you and your advisor don't do it, the markets will do it for you eventually.

Think of rebalancing as a kind of professional dollar-cost-averaging. When you rebalance, you're consistently, year after year, redirecting your profits towards the assets within your portfolio that offer the best value. People who don't rebalance their portfolios, will inevitably end up holding too much of an asset class at the wrong time and not enough at the right time.

Using the dynamic asset allocation technique, also helps to keep your schedule in order. Many people look after their investments in a haphazard way. When they're worried about them, they may choose to look them over, and when they think they see an opportunity, they may try to see if it fits. Industry professionals refer to this as investing based on greed and fear. In my humble opinion, it's one of the most common and costly mistakes individual investors make. Buying on greed and selling on fear is a vicious cycle and if you think about it, it really is just another way of saying "buy high and sell low."

Remember our chart showing the return of the average investor versus the return of the average mutual fund investor? Have another look.

AVERAGE STOCK FUND INVESTOR RETURN VS. AVERAGE STOCK FUND RETURN (1984-2000) (FIG. 22)

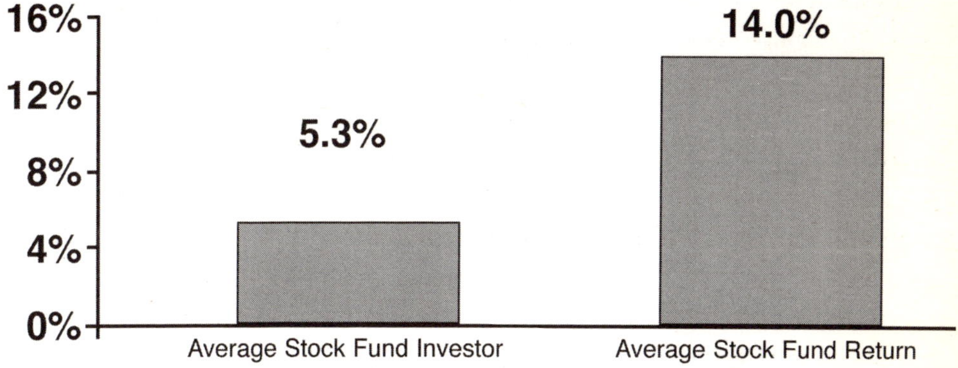

SOURCE: Dalbar Inc. and Lipper Inc.

The average investor has mastered the art of buying high and selling low. Every time these people touch their portfolios they do damage. Forget adding value, they are their own worst enemy. It'd be funny if we weren't talking about most of the adult population, but since we are, it's just sad.

Rebalancing your plan on a regular six-month schedule helps eliminate the possibility that this will happen to you. It should take less than four hours per year to do this, including the time you spend meeting or speaking with your advisor. That's probably less time than you spend now and trust me, the improved returns and lower risk will be more than worth your while.

The example that I'm including below is a little simplistic, but I think it'll help to highlight my point. Compare two hypothetical investment portfolios, both identically split between stocks and bonds. Both portfolios are invested fifty percent in bonds and fifty percent in stocks and both portfolios receive the same returns on both their stocks and bonds in year one and year two. In both examples, the cumulative returns for both the stocks and the bonds would be eight percent at the end of year two. The only difference between the two examples is that the first one is not rebalanced (in other words, it's left alone for the full two years), while in the second example, the portfolio is rebalanced back to its original asset allocation of fifty percent bonds and fifty percent stocks after the end of the first year.

FIGURE 23

DIVERSIFICATION EXAMPLE #1 — WITH NO REBALANCING

asset	start amount	start return	end year 1 amount	start year 2 amount	year 2 return	total end amount	2 year return
stocks	$10,000	20%	$12,000	$12,000	-10%	$10,800	8%
bonds	$10,000	-10%	$9,000	$9,000	20%	$10,800	8%
	$20,000	5%	$21,000	$21,000	5%	$21,600	8%

DIVERSIFICATION EXAMPLE #2 — WITH ANNUAL REBALANCING

asset	start amount	start return	end year 1 amount	rebalance back to 50/50 amount	year 2 return	total end amount	2 year return
stocks	$10,000	20%	$12,000	$10,500	-10%	$9,450	8%
bonds	$10,000	-10%	$9,000	$10,500	20%	$12,600	8%
	$20,000	5%	$21,000	$21,000	5%	$22,050	10.25%

At first glance, the two examples above may not make a lot of sense to you. Don't worry, very few people get this the first time through. If you don't understand why the cumulative total return was eight percent in the first example and 10.25 percent in the second example, then you probably forgot to consider the effect of compounding. The stocks and the bonds in both portfolios had a total return of eight percent over the two years. Naturally, in example #1 the unbalanced portfolio returns a total of eight percent (fifty percent of the portfolio was in bonds and they increased by eight percent, and fifty percent of the portfolio was in stocks, which also increased in value by eight percent).

In example #2 the rebalanced portfolio posts a total return of 10.25 percent. It posts the higher return because profits were taken from the stocks after year one and used to purchase more of the now cheaper bonds. Rebalancing forces us to sell high and buy low. Please allow me to take you through the rebalancing process in example #2. At the beginning, fifty percent of the portfolio is in stocks and fifty percent is invested in bonds (the same as the first example). At the end of year one, the stocks have risen in value and the bonds have dropped in value (again, this is the same as in the first example). Because of the rise in the value of the stocks and the drop in the value of the bonds, the portfolio is no longer a fifty-fifty mix. It's now comprised of $12,000 in stocks and $9,000 in bonds. In the second example, the portfolios were rebalanced back to their starting point of fifty percent stocks and fifty percent bonds. (To accomplish this, $1,500 worth of stocks are sold and $1,500 worth of bonds are bought, so that the portfolio now holds a total of $10,500 in stocks and bonds.) In the second year, the bonds gained twenty percent in value and the stocks dropped by ten percent. Because of the rebalancing, the portfolio in example #2 owned more of the bonds (which gained in value) and less of the stocks (which dropped in value) than the portfolio from the first example.

Please take another look at the two diversification examples above. I think you'll find they make a little more sense now.

The concept behind portfolio rebalancing isn't hard to grasp. Every six months, you sit down with or call your advisor and restore your portfolio back to the optimum pension asset allocation. The benefits are hard to ignore. Short-term volatility is reduced and long-term returns are improved. I told you these pension managers know what they're doing. The real question is, why aren't we all doing it?

Summary

- Using a technique called dynamic asset allocation, pension managers shave an additional ten to twenty percent off the already minimal risk level of the optimal portfolio. Dynamic asset allocation can also improve the long-term returns by about 2.5 percent.
- Dynamic asset allocation combats "portfolio drift," taking advantage of short-term volatility in the five major asset classes and their subclasses, in order to sell high and buy low.
- Rebalancing is a vital component of our asset allocation policy. What would be the point of knowing what the optimal pension portfolio looks like, if we didn't periodically ensure that our portfolio still reflects it?
- When it comes to rebalancing, I can assure you that if you and your advisor don't do it, the markets will do it for you eventually. People who don't rebalance inevitably end up holding too much of an asset class at the wrong time and not enough at the right time. Communicate with your advisor and review your portfolio twice per year.

Chapter Nine

Bringing Professional Help to Your Retirement Plan

Do not hire a man who does your work for money, but him who does it for love of it.

—Henry David Thoreau

Okay. So now you know what the optimal pension plan looks like. You know how it works and why it works. The only point we haven't covered is the actual investments themselves. I explained to you at the beginning of this book that the specific investments you choose won't have that much influence on whether or not you reach your financial goals. I stand by that. Dozens of studies have been done on investment performance. The exact results differ slightly from study to study, but the big picture is always the same: over ninety percent of your long-term returns are based on asset allocation. Remember this chart?

CONTRIBUTIONS TO LIFE-TIME INVESTMENT PERFORMANCE (FIG. 24)

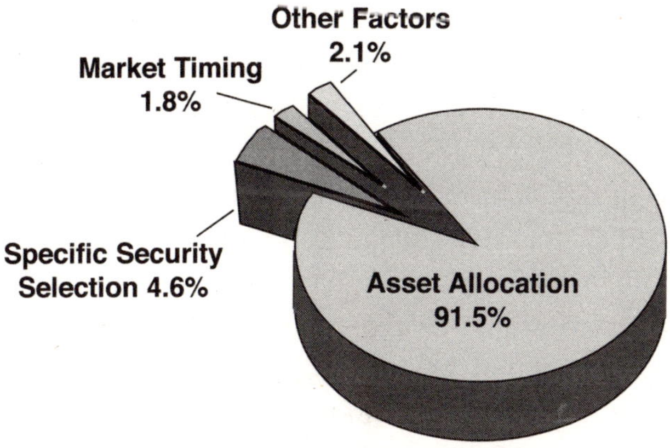

Source: Financial Analysts Journal, May/June 1991, "Determinants of Portfolio Performance II: An update" by Brinson, Singer and Beebower.

Modern portfolio theory is built on a foundation of asset allocation. The optimal pension portfolio uses modern portfolio theory to ensure that you receive the maximum returns that asset allocation can provide for you. If you use the optimal portfolio, you're over ninety percent of the way to a comfortable and safe retirement.

Dynamic asset allocation, or rebalancing, which we covered in the last chapter, eliminates the risk of market timing. As you can see above, market timing represents less than two percent of your total lifetime investment return. By combining the asset allocation of our optimum portfolio with regular semi-annual rebalancing, we can make sure that roughly ninety-four percent of the factors that contribute to your total lifetime investment returns are optimal.

We haven't even addressed specific investment selections yet and already ninety-four percent of the variability in your long-term returns has been tamed. I told you at the beginning of this book that the amount of risk and uncertainty in your portfolio could be slashed and we've done it.

So we agree that asset allocation and rebalancing are by far the most important part of your pension portfolio—about twenty times as important as the specific securities you buy—but still it's hard to completely ignore the individual investments. How do we continue to reduce and eliminate the risks in your portfolio, as we choose the specific positions you will own?

My answer to that question always has been, and always will be, professional management. I'm sure that some of you are do-it-yourself investors and I'm not going to try to change you. I'm just going to say two things. Number one, there are exactly twenty-seven distinct asset classes and subclasses in the optimal portfolio. If you want to properly diversify each of the twenty-seven classes, you need a minimum of twelve to twenty individual securities for each. That's a total of 300 to 500 individual positions. Do you really think you can handle that? I know I can't. Number two, every single one of the over 3,000 pension funds in North America hire professional investment managers to make their specific investment decisions. Every single one. If you want to enjoy the comfort and security the pension strategy offers, professional investment managers are a must.

Depending on the size of your investment portfolio, there are a few different ways you can go about hiring professional managers. If your portfolio is fairly large—more than a half-million dollars—then you may want to consider using some type of investment consulting service. Most major brokerage firms have access to an investment consulting service. Using this type of service, you can hire the premier managers in the world to handle each asset class in your portfolio; many of these are the same managers who run portfolios for the pension funds.

Investment consulting services offer three distinct advantages over other types of professional money management.

1. They offer access to the top investment managers in the world.

2. There are no costs associated with an investment consulting service, other than the annual management fee.

3. Your money is not pooled with the money of other investors.

Most amateur investors assume that mutual fund managers are the best professional investors out there. Some are very good, but they aren't necessarily the best. Part of the job description of a mutual fund manager is to sell themselves and the mutual fund to the public. As a result, mutual fund managers make themselves available for TV shows, newspaper and magazine articles and public speaking engagements. All this publicity acts to raise their profiles. Some mutual fund managers are practically household names, but just because someone is a household name, doesn't necessarily mean they're the best. Many great money managers toil in obscurity, helping pension funds, university endowments, charities and wealthy individuals.

As with any profession, the best tend to rise to the top and mammoth pension funds often represent the pinnacle of the money management field. Investment consulting services lump the considerable assets of their clients together and are thus able to meet the minimum investment demanded by virtually every professional money manager, mutual fund, pension or otherwise.

Investment consulting services charge an all-inclusive annual fee for their services. This fee represents the total cost of the service and it generally declines as the size of your portfolio increases. Because there are no other inbuilt costs, commissions or fees, this is generally the least expensive method of bringing professional money management to your personal pension plan.

It's also worth noting that with an investment consulting service, you have direct ownership over any securities purchased. Direct ownership affords your investment advisor greater flexibility in tax planning than pooled funds allow.

Unfortunately, most of you don't have more than a half-million dollars in your investment accounts and many of you have quite a bit less. Professional management is still available for you, but in order to obtain access to the best managers, you'll need to use a "pooled" fund. All pension funds are pooled, so I don't consider this to be any kind of disadvantage. Most of the major brokerage firms offer one or more pooled pension-style products; these are designed primarily for investment portfolios with a value of $100,000 or higher and they do the job very well. Pooled pension-style products, or wrap accounts as they're commonly called in the industry, are usually designed and managed under the supervision of an independent pension consulting firm. The pension consulting firm will select and hire one or more top quality managers for each asset class and subclass. The firm will continuously monitor the performance and decision-making process of the investment managers on an ongoing basis. When they deem it necessary, the independent pension consulting firm will fire or replace investment managers. They will then provide the investors with a written explanation of the reasoning behind the change. Similar to an investment consulting service, wrap accounts are subject to one all-inclusive fee and contain no hidden expenses or charges.

The only disadvantage with these vehicles is that currently none of them include the investment real estate or the absolute return asset classes. Still, they'll save you a ton of time and pooled funds are very flexible, allowing you to choose the exact percentages that will be placed in each asset class. You and your financial advisor can easily select good real estate and absolute return investments to complete your optimal asset allocation. The flexible nature of the pooled pension products will allow you to smoothly blend the five asset classes together in the proper proportions.

If you have less than $100,000 to work with, it's not a serious problem. There are still several pooled pension products available that will serve you well, but you'll find that you have less selection available to you than investors with larger portfolios. Several investment firms offer basic versions for young or new investors. The basic versions are virtually identical to the more advanced versions requiring higher minimum investments, the chief difference being less flexibility.

If you're just starting to save and can't yet meet the minimum investments of pooled funds, or if you have a little more time on your hands and want to spend more than a few hours a year on your pension plan, then mutual funds could be used to build your portfolio. As a general rule, you'll find the cost of management in a mutual fund portfolio slightly higher than the other two approaches. The primary reason is account size. The average mutual fund investor has a smaller portfolio than the average consulting or pooled fund client. A smaller account means incrementally higher costs for the fund company. It's also important to note that mutual funds don't usually give discounts for account size; whether you have $10,000 in a mutual fund portfolio or $10 million, the fee remains the same, as a percentage of your portfolio. In contrast, investment consulting services and pooled pension products, generally offer a sliding fee scale that decreases as the account grows in size. With a mutual fund portfolio, it can also be extremely difficult to ensure that each manager sticks to the asset class they should be covering. A value manager may decide to hold some growth investments or he may decide to hold some cash. These changes are out of your control and can have the effect of making your portfolio less optimal.

Regardless of the option that you ultimately select, professional management will have benefits. An optimal pension portfolio that utilizes professional management will almost certainly do at least an average job when it comes to specific security selection. This may not sound exciting, but consider that through our use of the optimal pension portfolio and dynamic asset allocation, we've already eliminated nearly ninety-four percent of the uncertainty from your lifetime investment return. By just doing an average job on specific security selection, we're eliminating more uncertainty. In fact, if we get just an average job from our professional managers while using the optimal pension asset allocation and semi-annual rebalancing, we will have eliminated close to ninety-seven percent of the uncertainty from your lifetime investment return.

It's not my intention to imply that you're only going to see average performance from your investment managers. On the contrary, if you enlist the help of a professional investment advisor, or even if you just take the time to choose managers wisely based on experience and quality, then it's extremely likely that you'll be the grateful beneficiary of significantly better-than-average performance. All I'm saying is that there's no need to bank on it. We can tame roughly ninety-seven percent of your uncertainty just by doing the basics. That's what pension funds concentrate on and that's what we should concentrate on.

I told you that we were going to slash the level of risk in your portfolio and we have. We added asset classes to your portfolio and took away risk. We added geographic diversification to your portfolio and took away risk. We diversified into subclasses—more risk gone. We started rebalancing twice a year—still more risk gone—and finally we added professional investment management to the mix. Goodbye risk. Each additional layer we added cut risk and increased the expected return in some way. I told you at the beginning of this book that there was no magic bullet. There isn't, but there is modern portfolio theory and it's a beautiful thing.

Working with a Professional Investment Advisor

You may have noticed that in this book, I've referred to your investment advisor several times. Some would say that it's presumptuous of me to assume that you're currently working with an investment advisor. I don't know if it's presumptuous of me, but I do know that I honestly don't believe anyone can do a better job managing their own retirement plan than they could do if they had a professional investment advisor working with them.

Before we go any further, I feel I should take the time to clarify the difference between an investment advisor and an investment manager. Both titles sound similar, so it's easy to get them confused, but it's important to differentiate, because they perform very different jobs for you. The investment advisor is the person you choose to work with in order to develop and ultimately implement and monitor your retirement plan. This is the person you select and hire. Hopefully you'll be working with them for a long time, so you should invest some effort making sure you've hired the right one. Investment managers, on the other hand, pick specific investments. They generally work with mutual funds, pension funds and investment consulting services. Your investment advisor should be very familiar with these investment managers and should be able to tell you which ones will do the best job of running each individual asset class within your plan.

The job of an investment advisor isn't picking the "hottest" or the best investments for you. Think about where the bulk of your lifetime investment returns come from. Over ninety percent come from asset allocation, so obviously a truly good advisor will spend the majority of his or her time ensuring that your portfolio does in fact conform to the optimal pension allocation as closely as possible. The skilled advisor will periodically rebalance your portfolio back to the optimal pension allocation, using the principle of dynamic asset allocation. By doing these two things, the skilled advisor is setting you up to finish ahead of the pack and putting you well on your way to achieving your financial goals.

By now, you've probably noticed that I don't have a lot of respect for investors or advisors who follow the crowd, jumping from one "hot" investment or investment manager to another. On the surface, it might seem to make sense to give your money to a manager who's doing very well. Consider this: over the past twenty years, you would've earned more money by investing with the managers who had the worst performance in the previous year than you would've made by investing with the so-called "hot" managers, those who had the best performance in the previous year. Investing in something that's hot is the same thing as buying high. Investors who subscribe to this method are buying high, hoping to sell higher. It just doesn't work. In the industry, we refer to this practice as "the greater fool theory"; one fool buys something in the hope that they can find an even bigger fool to take it off their hands at a profit.

Don't get me wrong, choosing high-quality investments is important, but the process with which these investments are selected is considerably more important than how they performed in the past year. The optimal pension portfolio contains twenty-seven different asset classes and subclasses. Twenty-seven is the optimal number to provide maximum diversification and minimum risk. These asset classes are not highly correlated to each other; if they were, they wouldn't offer diversification. Because they're not highly correlated, it's literally impossible for all or even most of these asset classes, and thus their managers, to be hot at the same time.

If your investment advisor is going to help you select the best quality managers for your pension plan, they need to have another way of assessing them besides performance. Ask your advisor what process they use to select managers (in the industry we refer to this process as due diligence). The best process for performing due diligence on an investment manager is to look at their strategy. Does it fit with your plan? If the strategy does fit with your plan, then you'd assess how good a job that manager does at sticking to her strategy. If an investment manager meets both of these criteria, then it's time to consider the quality of the team that provides her with the research she uses to make decisions and lastly, the long-term track record of the manager should be considered. As a side note, don't even bother considering any investment managers who lack a long-term track record. Let them learn their lessons with someone else's life savings.

As you set out on the journey to build financial security and comfort for your family, the first thing you need to address is the role of your investment advisor. If you're already working with an advisor who understands the importance of modern portfolio theory and dynamic asset allocation, then you've made a good start. The next question you have to ask yourself is: do I trust that this advisor has the best interests of myself and my family in mind at all times? If you're currently working with an advisor who understands and utilizes the principles of modern portfolio theory and dynamic asset allocation, and you're confident that he or she has your best interests in mind at all times, then you're fortunate. In the end, that's all you can really ask for.

If, on the other hand, you don't have a written investment plan that sets out your optimal asset allocation or you're not 100 percent sure that your advisor has your best interests in mind at all times, then it's time to start the search for a new one. In fact, I'm going to make that your first assignment.

Assignment #1: Find a skilled investment advisor to help you plan, design, implement, monitor and rebalance your personal pension plan.

Of the people reading this book, there may be a few who aren't working with an advisor. I respectfully submit that you're missing the point. There's only one acceptable reason for not working with a professional investment advisor—you haven't found the right one yet. Professional stock traders, pension fund managers, mutual fund managers, financial analysts, accountants, all these people use investment advisors.

Cost isn't a legitimate objection to using the services of a professional investment advisor. A skilled advisor will increase the total long-term returns of his clients by many times the fees they earn. Why? Because he'll make sure you actually stick to your plan, because he'll ensure your account is rebalanced at the appropriate time, because he'll hold your hand when you inevitably start to lose faith and most importantly, because he'll stop you from making stupid mistakes.

It may surprise you to learn this, but a professional advisor can actually get you discounts on investment expenses. Clients who work with advisors don't need to contact mutual fund companies or pension or investment managers directly, and don't require the same level of customer service from these firms as discount customers. Because of this, full service brokerage companies, which commonly have billions of client dollars invested with a single pension, mutual fund or investment manager, are able to negotiate steep management fee discounts for their clients. These discounts usually come in the form of a sliding fee scale, where costs decrease with account size. The price breaks usually occur at $100,000, $500,000 and $1,000,000 and continue in million-dollar increments.

I can't say this strongly enough: it's my firm belief that making use of the services of a skilled advisor will not only improve your returns, it will also reduce your risk. Remember, risk is really the chance that you'll fail to achieve your goals. You have a much better chance with a professional shoulder to lean on.

Summary

• The optimal pension portfolio uses modern portfolio theory to ensure that you target the maximum returns that asset allocation can provide for you. If you use the optimal portfolio, you're over ninety percent of the way to a comfortable and safe retirement.

• Combining dynamic asset allocation with the optimal pension portfolio ensures that roughly ninety-four percent of the factors that contribute to your total lifetime investment return are optimal.

• There are two reasons why I believe that your personal pension plan can only benefit from professional management. Firstly, 300 to 500 individual security positions is simply too many to manage effectively on your own. Secondly, every single one of the 3,000+ pension funds in North America makes use of professional investment managers. If you want to enjoy the comfort and security that the pension strategy offers, professional investment managers are a must.

• For investors with more than a half-million dollars available, the best value in professional money management is an investment consulting service. Most of the major full service brokerage firms in the US offer this type of service.

• If you currently have less than a half-million dollars available, a pooled pension-style fund should form the cornerstone of your personal pension plan. All pension funds are pooled, so I don't consider this a disadvantage.

• The costs associated with mutual funds are generally higher than investment consulting services and pooled funds. This applies even if the funds are purchased through a discount firm.

• An optimal pension portfolio that utilizes professional management and dynamic asset allocation, will almost certainly do at least an average job when it comes to specific security selection. This eliminates more uncertainty. In fact, when used together, these three strategies will eliminate close to ninety-seven percent of the uncertainly from your lifetime investment return.

• There's a difference between an investment advisor and an investment manager. The investment advisor is the person you select to work with in order to develop, implement and monitor your personal pension plan. Investment managers, on the other hand, pick specific investments. They generally work with mutual funds, pension funds and investment consulting services.

• I honestly don't believe that anyone can do a better job of managing their own retirement plan than a professional investment advisor could do for them.

• Your investment advisor's job is not to pick the hottest or best investments. His or her job is to monitor your plan on an ongoing basis, ensuring that your asset allocation is correct and that your investment managers are continuing to perform appropriately. Your advisor should be well-versed in the principle of dynamic asset allocation and should be alerting you when an opportunity to implement it presents itself. By doing these things, a skilled advisor is setting you up to finish ahead of the pack, putting you well on your way to achieving your financial goals.

• Choosing high-quality investments is important, but the process with which these investments are selected is considerably more important. This is referred to as performing your due diligence.

• If you're currently working with an investment advisor who provides you with a written investment plan and understands and utilizes the principles of modern portfolio theory and dynamic asset allocation, and you're confident that he or she has your best interests in mind at all times, then you're fortunate—hold on to that advisor for dear life. If not, it's time to find a new advisor.

• There's only one acceptable reason for not working with a professional investment advisor—you haven't found the right one yet.

• Because of economies of scale, a professional investment advisor at a large firm can actually get you discounts on investment expenses. These discounts usually come in the form of a sliding fee scale, where costs decrease with account size.

• If risk is the chance that you'll fail to achieve your goals, then a professional advisor reduces your risk. You have a much better chance with a professional shoulder to lean on.

CHAPTER TEN

Getting Started

The journey of a thousand miles begins with one step.
—Lao Tzu

As with everything in life, the first step is often the hardest. Planning your financial future is no exception. Maybe you've made some mistakes in the past or have been the recipient of some ill-timed or poorly conceived advice. It's time to put that behind you. You've already invested hours of your time learning about pension funds. If you create and stick to a well-designed plan, the pension strategy can and will work for you and your family. All you need to do is get started. I've prepared a step-by-step approach to help make this even easier for you. If you're currently working with an advisor, start with Step One; if not, move directly to Step Two.

Step One

Consider the relationship you have with your current financial advisor. Does he have your best interests in mind at all times? Does he understand your unique situation? Your financial goals and dreams? Does your current advisor understand and adhere to the principles of modern portfolio theory? If you aren't sure, give him a quick phone call and ask him to explain it to you. Is he actually rebalancing your account on a regular basis? Do you have to remind him or is he calling to remind you? These are the main tasks your advisor needs to perform for you. If he's doing them and more, great! Skip to Step Three. If not, it's time to move to Step Two.

Step Two

It's time to choose a financial advisor. In my opinion, the best way to find a skilled advisor is through word of mouth. Instigate conversations with your friends and family. Ask them how they feel about the advice they're getting. If they're happy, chances are there's a good reason. After you've gotten the names of two or three advisors, give them each a call and set up a meeting. Ask them about their education and any advanced financial designations they've earned. The CFP (Certified Financial Planner) and CIM (Certified Investment Manager) designations are a good start. Ask them to explain their investment and service philosophy to you. If the advisor doesn't adhere to the principles of modern portfolio theory and dynamic asset allocation, then keep looking. Make sure to ask prospective advisors about their experience. Don't ask how long they've been in the industry; ask specifically how long they've been working in an advisory capacity. As in any profession, some investment advisors are better than others, so take a few weeks and make sure you've picked one that you're comfortable with.

Selecting an investment advisor to place your trust in, is the most time consuming and most important step. From here on, everything is comparatively simple.

Step Three

This step is information gathering. In order to prepare a proper financial plan for you and the optimal portfolio that goes with it, your financial advisor is going to need some information.

a) Decide when you want to be able to retire. Note that I didn't ask when you're going to retire, but when you'd like to be able to, should you choose. Every pension plan knows when its members are eligible for retirement and your advisor must have access to the same information.

b) Make a list of how much income your family's producing now. How much do you want or expect in retirement? Write down your approximate monthly expenses. Divide your expenses between necessities and discretionary spending.

c) Gather all your latest statements concerning any investments you may own, any pension plans you're a member of through work and any life insurance policies you or your spouse own.

d) Make a list of your current assets (home, cottage, cars, etc.) and your current liabilities (mortgage, loans, line of credit, credit cards, etc.).

e) If you have a regular savings program in place, note how much you or your spouse is saving, how often and where it's currently being invested.

f) Dig out the latest tax returns for yourself and your spouse. Your new advisor will need them to sort out your 401k and IRA options and also to access opportunities for tax planning. (A dollar in tax saved is as good as two dollars earned and infinitely more satisfying.)

Gather this information together and be prepared to present it to your financial advisor at your next meeting.

Step Four

Sit down with your advisor. It's time to present him or her with all the information you've gathered. Together, you'll develop a lifelong plan that will act as a road map for your personal pension plan. Like a map, the plan should outline where you are now, where you want to end up and by when, and how you're going to get there. The plan should contain regular checkpoints, allowing you to evaluate your progress periodically, just as the great pension funds do. The plan should address your individual tax concerns, how much money you'll need to contribute in order to fund it, what type of returns you're targeting, what your margin for error is and of course, what your optimal pension portfolio looks like, as well as when your portfolio will be rebalanced using the principle of dynamic asset allocation.

Your completed financial plan should be a work of art. It will take your infinitely complex personal situation and reduce it to a simple process for you to follow. It will reduce the amount of tax you pay, cast light on your monthly spending habits (for better or for worse) and most importantly, if you stick to it, it will ensure you a safe, comfortable and financially worry-free retirement. Taking the time to have a top-quality financial plan prepared is one of the best investments you can ever make in your family's future.

Remember, your plan will only be as good as the information that went into its construction, so do the best you can when gathering the information in step three.

Step Five

Take your completed financial plan home and sleep on it. Reread it. Live with it for a week and see how you feel. It's not written in stone. Make a list of anything that you don't like or may not feel comfortable with. When the week is up, give your advisor a call and let him know. At this stage, a skilled advisor will easily be able to make adjustments to your plan to address any concerns you may have. Maybe it's just a few simple questions. Get your questions answered now. Your plan will work a heck of a lot better when you don't have any nagging concerns in the back of your mind.

Step Six

Step six is implementation. You've done your homework, you're now working with an advisor who inspires confidence and trust in you and your family, and you now have in your possession a working financial plan that will guide you through a safe and comfortable retirement. What are you waiting for? Give your advisor the go-ahead to get your pension plan started!

Step Seven

Now that you have your plan running, the lion's share of the work is done. The most important thing you can do now is give your plan the time and money it needs to get the job done for you. Together, you and your advisor should work out a schedule for carrying out the semi-annual rebalancing of your portfolio. Relax, live your life and enjoy your family. Your financial plan and your optimal pension portfolio will do its job—if you let it. Avoid the urge to tinker. In fact, I really don't see why you need to give any thought to your portfolio at all. Every six months, or whenever your plan dictates, have a conversation with your advisor and rebalance your portfolio back to your optimal design. Every year, on or near the anniversary of establishing your new plan, sit down with your advisor. Dig up your original copy of the plan and compare your present situation with the checkpoints originally established.

The day-to-day monitoring of your plan is your advisor's job. Delegate it to him or her and let them do their job. Just as I promised you in Chapter 1, once your pension portfolio is up and running, it will only require a few hours of your time per year.

You no longer have any excuses and you'll never again be able to tell yourself that you didn't know any better. Retirement planning is a tightrope act. If you want to provide long-term financial security for your family, then you must make a decision to include a moderate amount of short-term volatility in your portfolio now—not much, just about the same level as bonds should be plenty. If, despite the mountain of evidence beckoning you to the contrary, you opt for short-term security, do so knowing the price you'll surely pay. Decreased short-term risk translates to reduced long-term returns. In the world of pension plans, the only real risk is the risk that we won't achieve our goals. You're no different; the more you reduce your targeted returns, the greater the chance you'll fail to meet your goals. Ultimately, you can choose to eliminate short-term volatility or you can choose to eliminate long-term risk. You can't do both. As the old saying goes: pay me now or pay me later.

In Closing

People often refer to me as an eternal optimist and I suppose it's true. I believe with all my being that you hold the power within to put rational thought ahead of emotions like fear and greed. I challenge you to do just that. Take the knowledge I've given you and consider it with a rational mind. Choose the level of risk, and hence the target level of return, that gives your family the very best chance of seeing all their financial dreams come true. Volatility is an everyday fact of life, not a risk. There's going to be some volatility in any portfolio you choose. Instead of avoiding it, embrace it and profit through the principle of dynamic asset allocation. Choose the level of short-term volatility you're comfortable with and devote your efforts to ensuring that you're consistently targeting the maximum possible return on your hard-earned savings. These concepts are simple and they work. That's why pension funds have been using them for years.

Institutional investors, such as pension plans, achieve their goals about ninety percent of the time; only eleven percent of North American families can say the same thing. If anything's going to keep you up at night, this should be it, because it's the only real risk. The optimal portfolio has roughly the same amount of short-term volatility as bonds, yet it, in conjunction with a little discipline and a sound financial plan, virtually ensures your family will be one of the fortunate few who succeed. It really isn't going to get any better or any simpler than this.

You may not know everything there is to know about investing, but you do have all the tools you need to succeed. You know how to select and design your optimal portfolio and you know why it will work for you. It's up to you now. There's no reason why you can't make it happen.

Summary

• In life the first step in often the hardest; planning your financial future is no exception. It's time to put past mistakes or ill-conceived advice behind you.

• Getting started is as easy as seven simple steps:

1. Review the relationship with your current financial advisor.
2. Choose a financial advisor if you need one or need a new one.
3. Gather information.
4. Meet with your advisor and develop your pension strategy.
5. Take your completed plan home and sleep on it.
6. Implement your plan.
7. Monitor and rebalance your pension strategy on an ongoing basis.

• If you want to provide long-term financial security for your family, then you must make a decision to include a moderate amount of short-term volatility now. If, instead, you opt for short-term security, do so knowing the price you'll surely pay.

• Ultimately, you can choose to eliminate short-term volatility or you can choose to eliminate long-term risk. You can't do both. Pay now or pay later.

• I believe you hold the power within to put rational thought ahead of emotions like fear and greed. Don't avoid short-term volatility; choose to embrace it and profit from it instead. This is the strategy of the great pension plans.

Appendix: A Note on Standard Deviation

Harley Weston,
Department of Mathematics and Statistics,
University of Regina

Suppose you're in some course and have just received your grade on an exam. It's natural to ask how the rest of the class did on the exam, so you can put your grade in context. Knowing the mean or median, tells you the "center" or "middle" of the grades, but it would also be helpful to know some measure of the spread or variation in the grades.

Let's look at an example. Suppose three classes of five students each write the same exam and the grades are:

Class 1	Class 2	Class 3
82	82	67
78	82	66
70	82	66
58	42	66
42	42	65

Each of these classes has a mean, x, of 66, yet there's great difference in the variation of grades in each class. One measure of the variation is the range, which is the difference between the highest and lowest grades. In this example, the range for the first two classes is 40 (82 minus 42) while the range for the third class is 2 (67 minus 65). The range isn't a very good measure of variation here, as classes 1 and 2 have the same range, yet their variation seems to be quite different. One way to see this variation is to notice that in class 3 all the grades are very close to the mean, while in class 1 some grades are close to the mean and some are far away and in class 2 all the grades are a long way from the mean. It's this concept that leads to the definition of standard deviation.

Let's look at class 1. For each student, calculate the difference between the student's grade (x_1) and the mean.

Class 1	$x_1-\bar{x}$
82	16
78	12
70	4
58	-8
42	-24

The average of these differences could now be calculated as a measure of the variation, but this is zero. What's really needed is the distance from each grade to the mean, not the difference. You could take the absolute value of each difference and then calculate the mean. This is called the mean deviation, i.e., mean deviation $= \frac{\sum|x_1-\bar{x}|}{n}$, where n is the number of students in the class. For class

1 this is 12.8 (64 divided by 5). Another way to deal with the negative differences is to square each difference before adding.

Class 1	$x_1-\bar{x}$	$(x_1-\bar{x})^2$
82	16	256
78	12	144
70	4	16
58	-8	64
42	-24	576

The sum of this column is 1,056. To find what is called the standard deviation, s, divide this sum by n-1 and then, since the sum is in square units, take the square root. For class 1 this gives

$$s = \sqrt{\frac{\Sigma(x_1-\bar{x})^2}{n-1}} = \sqrt{\frac{1056}{4}} = 16.2$$

A similar calculation gives a standard deviation of 21.9 for class 2 and 0.7 for class 3. So, for class 3, where the grades are all close to the mean, the standard deviation is quite small; for class 1, where the grades are spread out between 42 and 82, the standard deviation is considerably larger; and for class 2, where all the grades are far from the mean, the standard deviation is larger still. The standard deviation is the quantity most commonly used by statisticians to measure the variation in a data set.

The formula for standard deviation is therefore: $\sigma = \sqrt{\frac{\Sigma(x_1-\mu)^2}{N}}$ (σ is the Greek letter sigma).

Glossary

absolute return investments: investments that yield or target a consistent real return, regardless of movement in the stock or bond markets.

actuarial tables: tools utilized by insurance companies to predict not who, but how many, out of a group of 1,000 people will die in any given year, as a function of age, sex and occupation.

asset allocation: the proportion in which capital is spread between the five major asset classes and their respective subclasses. The asset allocation decision consists of a balancing between risk and return.

asset class: a group of investments with similar characteristics. There are five major asset classes: cash, fixed-income, equity, real estate and absolute return.

basis point: used in reference to bonds, a basis point is 1/100 of one percent.

bear market: a major decline in stock or bond prices, defined as a twenty percent or greater drop in a key index.

bond: a security representing the repayment of principal at a certain date in the future (maturity date), plus the payment of a set amount of interest. A bond is a type of fixed-income or debt and the terms are used interchangeably.

bond ladder: a portfolio of bonds with staggered maturity dates, designed to eliminate interest rate risk and increase yields.

bull market: the opposite of a bear market. Defined as an increase in the value of stocks in excess of twenty percent since the previous low on the key indices.

capital market line: developed by James Tobin, the capital market line is a straight line on a graph of risk and return, beginning at the risk-free rate and running tangent to the efficient frontier. The point at which the line just touches a single point on the curve of the efficient frontier marks Tobin's super efficient portfolio, also referred to as the optimal pension portfolio.

Certificate of Deposit (CD): An FDIC insured fixed-income investment offered by banks and savings and loans. CDs are commonly considered by the general public to be the safest investment.

CFP: designates the bearer as a Certified Financial Planner, the highest level of planning achievement.

CIM: designates the bearer as a Certified Investment Manager. An advisor who has achieved this designation will understand the principles of modern portfolio theory and diversification.

conservative: investors who are primarily interested in preserving and increasing long-term real wealth, or investments that are helpful in preserving and increasing long-term wealth.

corporate bond: a bond issued by a corporation.

correlation: a statistical method used to indicate how closely two or more investments will react to the same external event.

CPI: the Consumer Price Index is a measurement of the rate of inflation in the United States.

currency risk: one of the five big risks, currency risk represents the chance that changes in the value of world currencies relative to the currency of your home country, will have an adverse effect on your investment portfolio.

diversification: the technique of spreading and subsequently lowering risk through purchasing different securities within the same asset class. Not to be confused with asset allocation.

dividend: a payment made to shareholders from a corporation's after-tax earnings. Because dividends are paid from after-tax earnings, they're given favorable tax treatment.

dynamic asset allocation: a method of neutralizing portfolio drift and improving returns. As the different asset classes change in value relative to each other, they are systematically restored to their original asset allocation. An investor using dynamic asset allocation, will consistently be selling high to buy low.

efficient frontier: on a graph of risk versus return, the efficient frontier is the line that passes through all optimal portfolios.

equity: represents equity ownership in a company. See stock.

equity mutual fund: a pooled fund that invests exclusively in stocks of public companies.

FDIC: The Federal Deposit Insurance Corporation is a federal agency that insures deposits in member institutions up to $100,000.

fixed-income: the asset class that includes all securities with fixed or guaranteed interest payments. Bonds, CDs, preferred shares and cash are all part of the fixed-income asset class and are commonly referred to collectively as "fixed-income."

foreign bonds: bonds issued by foreign governments or corporations.

government bond: a bond guaranteed by the federal or a municipal government.

gross domestic product or GDP: a measurement of the total value of a country's economy. Most commonly referred to in the media in the form of a percentage increase or decrease (e.g., US GDP is expected to increase by 2.5 percent next year).

growth stock: a stock that is valued by investors more for its ability to rapidly grow its earnings than for the underlying value of the company.

inflation risk: one of the five big risks, inflation risk represents the very real possibility that inflation will erode the purchasing power of an investor's money over time.

interest rate risk: one of the five big risks, interest rate risk can leave you stuck in low-yielding bonds or CDs at the wrong time.

investment advisor: the person you select to work with in order to develop, implement and monitor your investment plan. Some investment advisors are also qualified financial advisors and some are not—you need to ask.

investment manager: generally works with mutual funds, pension funds or investment consulting services. Decisions on specific security selection are usually made by the investment manager. Note the difference between an investment advisor and an investment manager.

liquid: large purchases or sales of liquid securities can be made quickly without significantly affecting the market price.

manager risk: see specific risk

market risk: one of the five big risks, market risk represents the chance that the value of your investments will decrease for no reason, other than the fact that other similar investments decreased in market value. Also known as systematic risk.

market timing: the act of purchasing or selling investments based primarily on short-term expectations of market movements. It doesn't work.

markets: a generic term encompassing all major stock markets (e.g., "The markets are doing well this year.").

modern portfolio theory: Harry Markowitz's Nobel Prize-winning theorem, says that for any given level of risk, there's only one portfolio of securities that will provide the maximum possible return. Conversely, for any given level of desired return, there exists only one portfolio that will exhibit the minimum possible amount of risk.

Municipal bond: A bond issued by a state or local government. Municipal bonds are backed by the full faith and credit of the issuer.

mutual fund: a pool of investors' money, managed by an investment company for a common purpose. The use of the word "fund" denotes that investor money is pooled.

optimal portfolio: the portfolio identified by James Tobin's capital market line. Also called the super efficient portfolio.

pension: a lifelong payment commencing at retirement that lasts until the death of the beneficiary or their spouse.

pension plan: the mechanism for managing the pool of money required to make good on the promised pension payments.

portfolio: the name given to all investment assets utilized for a common goal. An investor's retirement portfolio may be made up of securities in several different accounts.

portfolio drift: different asset classes tend to grow at different rates. Over time, if a portfolio isn't rebalanced, the fastest growing asset classes will begin to dominate. The most obvious example is that stocks grow faster than bonds over the long term.

preferred share: a member of the fixed-income asset class, preferred shares rate second to bonds in priority, however, they pay tax-advantaged dividend income as opposed to interest. Preferred shares are readily identifiable because they're issued in $25 increments and are usually listed on the stock exchange.

private pension plan: a pension plan without government support. A private pension plan is funded by contributions from the employer and the employees.

public pension plan: a government-sponsored pension scheme. Unlike a private pension plan, a public plan is not necessarily funded in advance. The government will often use contributions to fund current spending; future liabilities of the plan are left for the next generation to fund.

real return: a return after inflation. It represents the actual gain in purchasing power.

rebalancing: the effects of portfolio drift will cause an investment portfolio to become less efficient over time. Rebalancing restores the portfolio to its optimal asset allocation.

recession: a general contraction in the overall economic activity of the country, characterized by two consecutive quarters of declining GDP.

REIT: or Real Estate Investment Trust, is a publicly traded company that invests exclusively in real estate. REITs receive favorable tax treatment as long as a prescribed percentage of profits are distributed to unitholders annually.

risk: this book defines risk as the chance that you'll fail to achieve your goal.

risk-free rate: James Tobin introduced this concept in his capital market line theorem. The risk-free rate is defined as the maximum short-term rate of return an investor could be 100 percent confident of achieving. The ninety-day government

T-bill rate is usually used as a proxy for the risk-free rate.

S&P 500: Standard and Poor's composite index of 500 of the largest publicly traded stocks in the US. By market capitalization, it's the largest index of stocks in the world.

safety: the likelihood of conserving real purchasing power of money over a given period of time. In the short term, the safest investment for conserving purchasing power is government T-bills; in the long term, equities are the safest. The optimal pension portfolio offers the most efficient balance between these two extremes.

specific risk: one of the five big risks, specific risk is the risk associated with a specific investment or investment manager. Specific risk is one of the most dangerous types of risk. Fortunately, it's also one of the easiest to eliminate.

standard deviation: used in the investment world as a mathematical technique of expressing the short-term volatility of a portfolio in percentage terms. See Appendix 1.

stock: equity ownership of a corporation, represented by shares. The owners of stock have a *pro rata* claim on the corporation's earnings and assets. See equity.

systematic risk: see market risk.

the great pension plans: a generic term I created in order to encompass all the best private pension plans in North America.

value stock: a mature company valued by investors more for the underlying value of the company than for the ability to grow future earnings. See growth stock.

wrap account: a discretionary managed portfolio of stocks or pooled funds. Advisors using wrap accounts are not paid commissions; rather, they're paid fees based on a percentage of the value of the account.

yield: the annual interest or dividend payment of a security, divided by its current price. Not to be confused with yield to maturity.

yield to maturity: the total return of a fixed-income investment if held to maturity.

Index